Kaplan Publishing are constantly findir ways to make a difference to your stud exciting online resources really do offer something different to students looking for exam success.

This book comes with free MyKaplan online resources so that you can study anytime, anywhere

Having purchased this book, you have access to the following online study materials:

CONTENT	ACCA (including FFA,FAB,FMA)		AAT		FIA (excluding FFA,FAB,FMA)	
	Text	Kit	Text	Kit	Text	Kit
iPaper version of the book	✓	✓	✓	✓	✓	✓
Interactive electronic version of the book	✓					
Progress tests with instant answers	✓		✓			
Mock assessments online			✓	✓		
Material updates	✓	✓	✓	✓	✓	✓
Latest official ACCA exam questions		✓				
Extra question assistance using the signpost icon*		✓				
Timed questions with an online tutor debrief using the clock icon*		✓				
Interim assessment including questions and answers	✓				✓	
Technical articles	✓	✓			✓	✓

* Excludes F1, F2, F3, FFA, FAB, FMA

How to access your online resources

Kaplan Financial students will already have a MyKaplan account and these extra resources will be available to you online. You do not need to register again, as this process was completed when you enrolled. If you are having problems accessing online materials, please ask your course administrator.

If you are already a registered MyKaplan user go to www.MyKaplan.co.uk and log in. Select the 'add a book' feature and enter the ISDN number of this book and the unique pass key at the bottom of this card. Then click 'finished' or 'add another book'. You may add as many books as you have purchased from this screen.

If you purchased through Kaplan Flexible Learning or via the Kaplan Publishing website you will automatically receive an e-mail invitation to MyKaplan. Please register your details using this email to gain access to your content. If you do not receive the e-mail or book content, please contact Kaplan Flexible Learning.

If you are a new MyKaplan user register at www.MyKaplan.co.uk and click on the link contained in the email we sent you to activate your account. Then select the 'add a book' feature, enter the ISBN number of this book and the unique pass key at the bottom of this card. Then click 'finished' or 'add another book'.

Your Code and Information

This code can only be used once for the registration of one book online. This registration and your online content will expire when the final sittings for the examinations covered by this book have taken place. Please allow one hour from the time you submit your book details for us to process your request.

Please scratch the film to access your MyKaplan code.

Please be aware that this code is case-sensitive and you will need to include the dashes within the passcode, but not when entering the ISBN. For further technical support, please visit www.MyKaplan.co.uk

ACCA

Paper F3

FIA

Diploma in Accounting and Business

Financial Accounting (FA/FFA)

EXAM KIT

British Library Cataloguing-in-Publication Data

A catalogue record for this book is available from the British Library.

Published by:

Kaplan Publishing UK

Unit 2 The Business Centre

Molly Millar's Lane

Wokingham

Berkshire

RG41 2QZ

ISBN: 978-0-85732-824-3

© Kaplan Financial Limited, 2013

Printed and bound in Great Britain

Acknowledgements

The past ACCA examination questions are the copyright of the Association of Chartered Certified Accountants. The original answers to the questions from June 1994 onwards were produced by the examiners themselves and have been adapted by Kaplan Publishing.

We are grateful to the Chartered Institute of Management Accountants and the Institute of Chartered Accountants in England and Wales for permission to reproduce past examination questions. The answers have been prepared by Kaplan Publishing.

CONTENTS

	Page
Index to questions and answers	v
Exam Technique	vii
Paper specific information	ix
Kaplan's recommended revision approach	xi

Section

1	Multiple choice test questions	1
2	Multi-task questions	83
3	Answers to multiple choice test questions	93
4	Answers to Multi-task questions	157
5	ACCA Specimen examination paper	

 New features in this edition

In addition to providing a wide ranging bank of practice questions, we have also included in this edition:

- Details of the new format examination, effective from February 2014.
- Examples of new style 'multi task' questions that will form part of the new examination format.
- Paper specific information and advice on exam technique.
- Our recommended approach to make your revision for this particular subject as effective as possible.

  This includes step by step guidance on how best to use our Kaplan material (Complete text, pocket notes and exam kit) at this stage in your studies.

You will find a wealth of other resources to help you with your studies on the following sites:

www.EN-gage.co.uk and www.accaglobal.com/students/

INDEX TO QUESTIONS AND ANSWERS

MULTIPL CHOICE TEST QUESTIONS

	Page number	
	Question	Answer
Introduction to financial reporting	1	93
Statement of financial position and statement of profit or loss	3	94
Double entry bookkeeping	5	96
Inventory	8	98
Sales tax	13	102
Accruals and prepayments	15	104
Irrecoverable debts and allowances for receivables	19	106
Non-current assets	23	111
From trial balance to financial statements	29	116
Books of prime entry and control accounts	34	120
Control account reconciliations	37	122
Bank reconciliations	40	125
Correction of and errors suspense accounts	45	130
Incomplete records	51	136
Company accounts	56	140
Accounting standards	61	144
Statement of cash flows	65	146
Regulatory framework	70	150
Group financial statements	73	152
Interpretation of financial statements	79	155

MULTI-TASK QUESTIONS

	Page number	
	Question	Answer
Ice	83	157
Willow	84	159
Clerc	85	162
Carbon	86	165
Patty and Selma	87	166
Cube and Prism	88	168
Bryson and Stoppard	89	170
Pen and Staple	90	171
Pebble and Stone	91	173

EXAM TECHNIQUE

- **Do not skip any of the material** in the syllabus.

- **Read each question** *very* carefully.

- **Double-check your answer** before committing yourself to it.

- Answer **every** question – if you do not know an answer, you don't lose anything by guessing. Think carefully before you **guess**. The examiner has indicated that many candidates are still leaving blank answers in the real exam.

- If you are answering a multiple-choice question, **eliminate first those answers that you know are wrong**. Then choose the most appropriate answer from those that are left.

- Remember that **only one answer to a multiple-choice question can be right**. After you have eliminated the ones that you know to be wrong, if you are still unsure, guess. Only guess after you have double-checked that you have only eliminated answers that are *definitely* wrong.

- **Don't panic** if you realise you've answered a question incorrectly. Getting one question wrong will not mean the difference between passing and failing

Computer-based exams – tips

- Do not attempt a CBE until you have **completed all study material** relating to it.

- On the ACCA website there is a CBE demonstration. It is **ESSENTIAL** that you attempt this before your real CBE. You will become familiar with how to move around the CBE screens and the way that questions are formatted, increasing your confidence and speed in the actual exam.

- Be sure you understand how to use the **software** before you start the exam. If in doubt, ask the assessment centre staff to explain it to you.

- Questions are **displayed on the screen** and answers are entered using keyboard and mouse. At the end of the exam, you are given a certificate showing the result you have achieved.

- In addition to the traditional multiple-choice question type, CBEs might also contain **other types of questions**, such as number entry questions, formula entry questions, and stem questions with multiple parts.

- You need to be sure you **know how to answer questions** of this type before you sit the exam, through practice.

PAPER SPECIFIC INFORMATION

THE EXAM

FORMAT OF THE PAPER-BASED AND COMPUTER-BASED EXAM

	Number of marks
35 compulsory multiple-choice questions (2 marks each)	70
2 multi-task questions (15 marks each)	30

Total time allowed: 2 hours

- Two mark questions will usually comprise the following answer types:

    (i)   Multiple choice with four options (A, B, C or D)

    (ii)   Ask you to select two correct answers from a choice of four

- The multi-task questions will test consolidations and accounts preparation. The consolidation question could include a small amount of interpretation.

- The examinations contain 100% compulsory questions and students must study across the breadth of the syllabus to prepare effectively for the examination

- The examination will be assessed by a two hour paper-based or computer-based examination

PASS MARK

The pass mark for all ACCA Qualification examination papers is 50%.

DETAILED SYLLABUS

The detailed syllabus and study guide written by the ACCA can be found at:

www.accaglobal.com/students/

KAPLAN'S RECOMMENDED REVISION APPROACH

QUESTION PRACTICE IS THE KEY TO SUCCESS

Success in professional examinations relies upon you acquiring a firm grasp of the required knowledge at the tuition phase. In order to be able to do the questions, knowledge is essential.

However, the difference between success and failure often hinges on your exam technique on the day and making the most of the revision phase of your studies.

The **Kaplan complete text** is the starting point, designed to provide the underpinning knowledge to tackle all questions. However, in the revision phase, pouring over text books is not the answer.

Kaplan online progress tests help you consolidate your knowledge and understanding and are a useful tool to check whether you can remember key topic areas.

Kaplan pocket notes are designed to help you quickly revise a topic area, however you then need to practice questions. There is a need to progress to full exam standard questions as soon as possible, and to tie your exam technique and technical knowledge together.

The importance of question practice cannot be over-emphasised.

The recommended approach below is designed by expert tutors in the field, in conjunction with their knowledge of the examiner.

The approach taken for the fundamental papers is to revise by topic area.

You need to practice as many questions as possible in the time you have left.

OUR AIM

Our aim is to get you to the stage where you can attempt exam standard questions confidently, to time, in a closed book environment, with no supplementary help (i.e. to simulate the real examination experience).

Practising your exam technique on real past examination questions, in timed conditions, is also vitally important for you to assess your progress and identify areas of weakness that may need more attention in the final run up to the examination.

The approach below shows you which questions you should use to build up to coping with exam standard question practice, and references to the sources of information available should you need to revisit a topic area in more detail.

Remember that in the real examination, all you have to do is:

- attempt all questions required by the exam

- only spend the allotted time on each question, and

- get them at least 50% right!

Try and practice this approach on every question you attempt from now to the real exam.

THE KAPLAN PAPER F3 REVISION PLAN

Stage 1: Assess areas of strengths and weaknesses

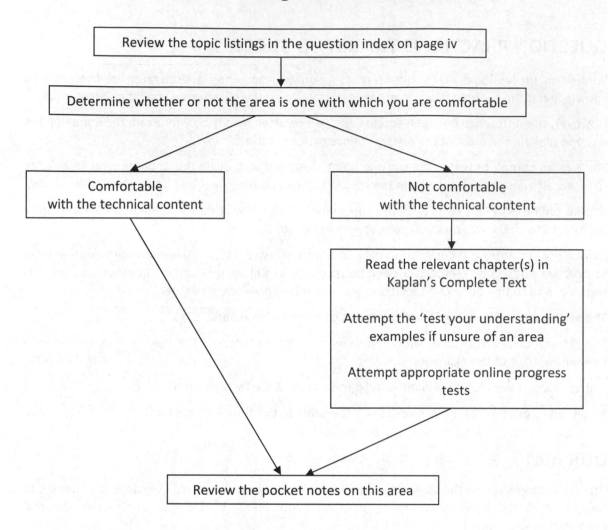

Stage 2: Practice questions

Ensure that you revise all syllabus areas as questions could be asked on anything.

Try to avoid referring to text books and notes and the model answer until you have completed your attempt.

Try to answer the question in the allotted time.

Review your attempt with the model answer. If you got the answer wrong, can you see why? Was the problem a lack of knowledge or a failure to understand the question fully?

Fill in the self-assessment box below and decide on your best course of action.

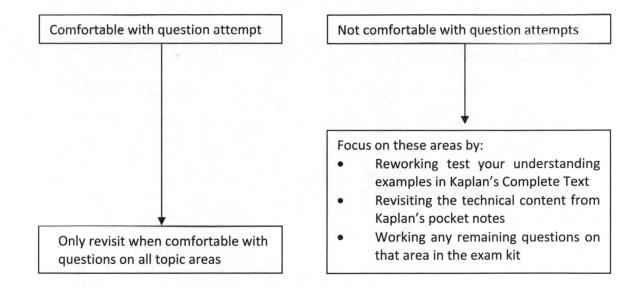

Stage 3: Final pre-exam revision

We recommend that you **attempt at least one two hour mock examination** containing a set of previously unseen exam standard questions.

It is important that you get a feel for the breadth of coverage of a real exam without advanced knowledge of the topic areas covered – just as you will expect to see on the real exam day.

Ideally this mock should be sat in timed, closed book, real exam conditions and could be:

- a mock examination offered by your tuition provider, and/or

- the pilot paper in the back of this exam kit, and/or

- the practice simulation paper in this kit

Section 1

MULTIPLE CHOICE TEST QUESTIONS

INTRODUCTION TO FINANCIAL REPORTING

1 **Which of the following statements is true?**

A   The directors of a company are liable for any losses of the company

B   A sole trader business is owned by shareholders and operated by the proprietor

C   Partners are liable for losses in a partnership in proportion to their profit share ratio

D   A company is run by directors on behalf of its members **(2 marks)**

2 **Which of the following best describes management accounts?**

A   Management accounts are mandatory accounts which reflect the past performance of a business and are prepared in accordance with strict accounting requirements

B   Management accounts are normally prepared monthly on a rolling basis and include details of past performance as well as budgets and forecasts

C   Management accounts are required by law and include sufficient detail for managers control the business and prepare for the future

D   Management accounts include information computed to be relevant to managers and are generally prepared annually **(2 marks)**

3 **Which of the following best explains why employees are interested in the financial statements of their employer?**

A   To compare the business with its competitors in order to decide whether to seek employment with one of those competitors

B   To assess the effect of the business on the local economy, community and environment

C   To assess whether the business will continue into the foreseeable future

D   To assess the profitability of the business in order to decide whether to invest in it **(2 marks)**

4 **Which of the following user groups require the most detailed financial information?**

A   The management

B   Investors and potential investors

C   Government agencies

D   Employees   **(2 marks)**

5 **Which of the following statements are true?**

1   Accounting can be described as the recording and summarising of transactions.

2   Financial accounting describes the production of a statement of financial position and statement of profit or loss for internal use.

A   1 only

B   2 only

C   Both 1 and 2

D   None   **(2 marks)**

6 **The main aim of financial accounting is to:**

A   record all transactions in the books of account

B   provide management with detailed analyses of costs

C   present the financial results to the organisation by means of recognised statements

D   calculate profit   **(2 marks)**

7 **Which one of the following sentences does NOT explain the distinction between financial accounts and management accounts?**

A   Financial accounts are primarily for external users and management accounts are primarily for internal users

B   Financial accounts are normally produced annually and management accounts are normally produced monthly

C   Financial accounts are more accurate than management accounts

D   Financial accounts are audited by an external auditor and management accounts do not normally have an external audit   **(2 marks)**

STATEMENT OF FINANCIAL POSITION AND STATEMENT OF PROFIT OR LOSS

8   The following information relates to Minnie's hairdressing business in the year ended 31 August 20X7:

	$
Expenses	7,100
Opening inventory	1,500
Closing inventory	900
Purchases	12,950
Gross profit	12,125
Inventory drawings of shampoo	75

What is the sales figure for the business?

A $32,700

B $25,600

C $25,675

D $25,750   (2 marks)

9   An asset is:

A   An item owned by an entity

B   An item controlled by an entity

C   An amount that is owed by the entity

D   A short term liability   (2 marks)

10 Arthur had net assets of $19,000 at 30 April 20X7. During the year to 30 April 20X7, he introduced $9,800 additional capital into the business. Profits were $8,000, of which he withdrew $4,200.

What was the balance on Arthur's capital account at 1 May 20X6?

A $5,400

B $13,000

C $16,600

D $32,600   (2 marks)

11 The capital of a business would change as a result of:

A   a supplier being paid by cheque

B   raw materials being purchased on credit

C   non-current assets being purchased on credit

D   wages being paid in cash   (2 marks)

12 A draft statement of financial position has been prepared for Lollipop, a sole trader. It is now discovered that a loan due for repayment by Lollipop fourteen months after the reporting date has been included in trade payables.

The necessary adjustment will:

A have no effect on net current assets

B increase net current assets

C reduce net current assets

D increase current assets but reduce net current assets **(2 marks)**

13 The profit of a business may be calculated by using which one of the following formulae?

A Opening capital – drawings + capital introduced – closing capital

B Closing capital + drawings – capital introduced – opening capital

C Opening capital + drawings – capital introduced – closing capital

D Closing capital – drawings + capital introduced – opening capital **(2 marks)**

14 Which accounting concept requires that amounts of goods taken from inventory by the proprietor of a business are treated as drawings?

A Accruals

B Prudence

C Separate entity

D Substance over form **(2 marks)**

15 The following information is available about Andrew's business at 30 September 20X6:

	$
Motor van	14,000
Loan (repayable in 4 equal annual instalments starting 1 January 20X7)	100,000
Receivables	23,800
Bank balance (a debit on the bank statement)	3,250
Accumulated depreciation	7,000
Payables	31,050
Inventory	12,560
Petty cash	150
Rent due	1,200
Allowance for receivables	1,500

What are the correct figures for current liabilities and current assets?

	Current liabilities	Current assets
	$	$
A	34,300	35,010
B	32,250	38,260
C	57,250	38,260
D	60,500	35,010

(2 marks)

16 **The following transactions relate to Max's business:**

1 May	Purchase of goods for resale on credit	$300
2 May	Max injects long term capital into the business	$1,400
3 May	Payment of rent made	$750
5 May	Max withdraws cash from the business	$400
7 May	Sales made on credit	$1,200

(goods originally cost $600)

At the start of the week, the assets of the business were $15,700 and liabilities amounted to $11,200.

At the end of the week, what is the amount of Max's capital?

A $5,350

B $1,400

C $850

D $1,000 **(2 marks)**

DOUBLE ENTRY BOOKKEEPING

17 **Oscar runs a sole trader business selling computers. On 12 January 20X7, he employed his daughter as an administrator for the business and took a computer from the store room for her to use in the office.**

What is the double entry for this transaction?

A	Dr Drawings	Cr Cost of sales
B	Dr Non-current assets	Cr Cost of sales
C	Dr Cost of sales	Cr Drawings
D	Dr Cost of sales	Cr Non-current assets

(2 marks)

18 **Which of the following items appear on the same side of the trial balance?**

A Drawings and accruals

B Carriage outwards and prepayments

C Carriage inwards and rental income

D Opening inventory and purchase returns **(2 marks)**

19 **The double-entry system of book-keeping normally results in which of the following balances on the ledger accounts?**

	Debit balances:	*Credit balances:*
A	Assets and revenues	Liabilities, capital and expenses
B	Revenues, capital and liabilities	Assets and expenses
C	Assets and expenses	Liabilities, capital and revenues
D	Assets, expenses and capital	Liabilities and revenues

(2 marks)

20   The most important reason for producing a trial balance prior to preparing the final accounts is:

A   it confirms the accuracy of the ledger accounts

B   it provides all the figures necessary to prepare the final accounts

C   it shows that the ledger accounts contain debit and credit entries of an equal value

D   it enables the accountant to calculate any adjustments required   **(2 marks)**

21   **Sasha has prepared a draft statement of profit or loss for her business:**

	$	$
Sales		256,800
Cost of sales		
Opening inventory	13,400	
Purchases	145,000	
Closing inventory	(14,200)	
		(144,200)
Gross profit		112,600
Expenses		(76,000)
Net profit		36,600

Sasha has not yet recorded the following items:

- Carriage in of $2,300

- Discounts received of $3,900

- Discounts allowed of $1,950

After these amounts are recorded, what are the revised gross and net profits of Sasha's business?

	Gross profit	Net profit
	$	$
A	108,350	36,250
B	108,350	28,450
C	110,300	28,450
D	110,300	36,250

                                                                                      (2 marks)

22 Elijah started the month with a positive balance of $1,780 on his bank account. What is the balance after the following transactions in June?

1 Elijah withdraws $200 per week to cover living expenses.

2 A settlement discount of $30 is taken by a customer on a sale of $600.

3 An amount of $400 is received from a credit customer.

4 Bankings of $1,200 from petty cash.

A $3,750

B $3,150

C $3,180

D $2,580 **(2 marks)**

23 After corrections, what should be the balance on the following account?

Bank

	$		$
Overdraft at start of month	1,340	Returns of goods purchased for cash	50
Reimbursement of petty cash float	45	Payments to credit suppliers	990
Receipts from customers	4,400	Rental income	1,300
		Payment of electricity bill	700
		Balance c/f	2,745
	5,785		5,785

A $2,665

B $2,765

C $5,345

D $2,675 **(2 marks)**

24 Andrea started a taxi business by transferring her car, worth $5,000, into the business.

What are the accounting entries required to record this?

A Dr Capital $5,000, Cr Car $5,000

B Dr Car $5,000, Cr Drawings $5,000

C Dr Car $5,000, Cr Capital $5,00

D Dr Drawings, Cr Car **(2 marks)**

INVENTORY

25   An item of inventory was purchased for $500. It is expected to be sold for $1,200 although $250 will need to be spent on it in order to achieve the sale. To replace the same item of inventory would cost $650. How should the inventory be valued in the accounts?

A $500

B $750

C $950

D $650   (2 marks)

26   Appleby buys and sells inventory during the month of August as follows:

Opening inventory		100 units	$2.52/unit
4 August	Sales	20 units	
8 August	Purchases	140 units	$2.56/unit
10 August	Sales	90 units	
18 August	Purchases	200 units	$2.78/unit
20 August	Sales	180 units	

The periodic weighted average for the month is calculated as follows:

Total value of inventory (opening inventory plus purchase costs during the month) divided by total units (opening inventory plus purchase costs during the month).

Which of the following statements is true?

A   Closing inventory is $19.50 higher when using the FIFO method instead of the periodic weighted average

B   Closing inventory is $19.50 lower when using the FIFO method instead of the periodic weighted average

C   Closing inventory is $17.50 higher when using the FIFO method instead of the periodic weighted average

D   Closing inventory is $17.50 lower when using the FIFO method instead of the periodic weighted average   (2 marks)

27   In the year ended 31 August 20X4, Aplus' records show closing inventory of 1,000 units compared to 950 units of opening inventory. Which of the following statements is true assuming that prices have fallen throughout the year?

A   Closing inventory and profit are higher using FIFO rather than AVCO.

B   Closing inventory and profit are lower using FIFO rather than AVCO.

C   Closing inventory is higher and profit lower using FIFO rather than AVCO.

D   Closing inventory is lower and profit higher using FIFO rather than AVCO.

(2 marks)

28 David performs an inventory count on 30 December 20X6 ahead of the 31 December year end. He counts 1,200 identical units, each of which cost $50. On 31 December, David sold 20 of the units for $48 each. What figure should be included in David's statement of financial position for inventory at the year end?

A $60,000

B $59,000

C $57,600

D $56,640   **(2 marks)**

29 Which of the following statements about the treatment of inventory and work in progress in financial statements are correct?

(1)   Inventory should be valued at the lower of cost, net realisable value and replacement cost.

(2)   In valuing work in progress, materials costs, labour costs and variable and fixed production overheads must be included.

(3)   Inventory items can be valued using either first in, first out (FIFO) or weighted average cost.

(4)   A company's financial statements must disclose the accounting policies used in measuring inventories.

A   All four statements are correct

B   (1), (2) and (3) only

C   (2), (3) and (4) only

D   (1) and (4) only   **(2 marks)**

30 Kiera's interior design business received a delivery of fabric on 29 June 20X6, which was included in inventory at 30 June 20X6. The invoice for the goods was recorded in July 20X6.

What effect will this have on the business?

(1)   Profit for the year ended 30 June 20X6 will be overstated.

(2)   Inventory at 30 June 20X6 will be understated.

(3)   Profit for the year ended 30 June 20X7 will be overstated.

(4)   Inventory at 30 June 20X6 will be overstated.

A   (1) and (2)

B   (2) and (3)

C   (1) only

D   (1) and (4)   **(2 marks)**

31   What journal entry is required to record goods taken from inventory by the owner of a business for personal use?

    A   Dr Drawings   Cr Purchases

    B   Dr Sales   Cr Drawings

    C   Dr Drawings   Cr Inventory

    D   Dr Inventory   Cr Drawings   **(2 marks)**

32   A business had an opening inventory of $180,000 and a closing inventory of $220,000 in its financial statements for the year ended 31 December 20X5.

Which of the following entries for these opening and closing inventory figures are made when completing the financial records of the business?

		Debit	Credit
		$	$
A	Inventory account	180,000	
	Statement of profit or loss		180,000
	Statement of profit or loss	220,000	
	Inventory account		220,000
B	Statement of profit or loss	180,000	
	Inventory account		180,000
	Inventory account	220,000	
	Statement of profit or loss		220,000
C	Inventory account	40,000	
	Purchases account		40,000
D	Purchases account	40,000	
	Inventory account		40,000

                                                                   (2 marks)

33   Ajay's annual inventory count took place on 7 July 20X6. The inventory value on this date was $38,950. During the period from 30 June 20X6 to 7 July 20X6, the following took place:

Sales $6,500

Purchases $4,250

The mark up is 25% on cost.

What is Ajay's inventory value at 30 June 20X6?

    A $38,000

    B $39,900

    C $41,200

    D $39,575   **(2 marks)**

34 **Inventory movements for product X during the last quarter were as follows:**

Opening inventory at 1 January was 6 items valued at $15 each.

January	Purchases	10 items at $19.80 each
February	Sales	10 items at $30 each
March	Purchases	20 items at $24.50
	Sales	5 items at $30 each

Gross profit for the quarter, using the continuous weighted average cost method, would be:

A $135.75

B $155.00

C $174.00

D $483.00

(2 marks)

35 **Your firm values inventory using the weighted average cost method. At 1 October 20X8, there were 60 units in inventory valued at $12 each. On 8 October, 40 units were purchased for $15 each, and a further 50 units were purchased for $18 each on 14 October. On 21 October, 75 units were sold for $1,200.**

The value of closing inventory at 31 October 20X8 was:

A $900

B $1,020

C $1,110

D $1,125

(2 marks)

36 **Percy Pilbeam is a book wholesaler. On each sale, commission of 4% is payable to the selling agent.**

The following information is available in respect of total inventories of three of his most popular titles at his financial year-end:

	Cost	Selling price
	$	$
Henry VII – Shakespeare	2,280	2,900
Dissuasion – Jane Armstrong-Siddeley	4,080	4,000
Pilgrim's Painful Progress – John Bunion	1,280	1,300

What is the total value of these inventories in Percy's statement of financial position?

A $7,368

B $7,400

C $7,560

D $7,640

(2 marks)

37 An organisation's inventory at 1 July is 15 units at a cost of $3.00 each. The following movements occur:

3 July 20X4   5 units sold at $3.30 each

8 July 20X4   10 units bought at $3.50 each

12 July 20X4   8 units sold at $4.00 each

Closing inventory at 31 July, using the FIFO method of inventory valuation, would be

A $31.50

B $36.00

C $39.00

D $41.00   **(2 marks)**

38 What would be the effect on a company's profit of discovering inventory with cost of $1,250 and a net realisable value of $1,000, assuming that the same inventory had not been included in the original inventory count?

A   An increase of $1,250

B   An increase of $1,000

C   A decrease of $250

D   No effect at all   **(2 marks)**

39 S & Co sell three products – Basic, Super and Luxury. The following information was available at the year end:

	Basic	Super	Luxury
	$ per unit	$ per unit	$ per unit
Original cost	6	9	18
Estimated selling price	9	12	15
Selling and distribution costs	1	4	5
	units	units	units
Units in inventory	200	250	150

The value of inventory at the year end should be:

A $4,200

B $4,700

C $5,700

D $6,150   **(2 marks)**

40   In times of rising prices, the valuation of inventory using the First In First Out method, as opposed to the Weighted Average Cost method, will result in which ONE of the following combinations?

	Cost of sales	Profit	Closing inventory
A	Lower	Higher	Higher
B	Lower	Higher	Lower
C	Higher	Lower	Higher
D	Higher	Higher	Lower

(2 marks)

SALES TAX

41   Erin is registered for sales tax. During May, she sells goods with a tax exclusive price of $600 to Kyle on credit. As Kyle is buying a large quantity of goods, Erin reduces the price by 5%. She also offers a discount of another 3% if Kyle pays within 10 days. Kyle does not pay within the 10 days.

If sales tax is charged at 17.5%, what amount should Erin charge on this transaction?

A $96.76

B $101.85

C $99.75

D $105.00

(2 marks)

42   At 1 December 20X5, Laurel owes the sales tax authorities $23,778. During the month of December, she recorded the following transactions:

•   Sales of $800,000 exclusive of 17.5% sales tax.

•   Purchases of $590,790 inclusive of sales tax.

What is the balance on Laurel's sales tax account at the end of December?

A $54,937

B $60,389

C $75,788

D $163,778

(2 marks)

43   If sales (including sales tax) amounted to $27,612.50, and purchases (excluding sales tax) amounted to $18,000, the balance on the sales tax account, assuming all items are subject to tax at 17.5%, would be:

A $962.50 Dr

B $962.50 Cr

C $1,682.10 Dr

D $1,682.10 Cr

(2 marks)

44   In the quarter ended 31 March 20X2, Chas had taxable sales, net of sales tax, of $90,000 and taxable purchases, net of sales tax, of $72,000.

If the rate of sales tax is 10%, how much sales tax is due?

A $1,800 receivable

B $2,000 receivable

C $1,800 payable

D $2,000 payable   (2 marks)

45   A summary of the transactions of Ramsgate, who is registered for sales tax at 17.5%, shows the following for the month of August 20X9.

Outputs $60,000 (exclusive of tax)

Inputs $40,286 (inclusive of tax)

At the beginning of the period Ramsgate owed $3,400 to the authorities, and during the period he has paid $2,600 to them.

At the end of the period the amount owing to the authorities is:

A $3,700

B $3,930

C $4,400

D $5,300.   (2 marks)

46   The sales account is:

A   credited with the total of sales made, including sales tax

B   credited with the total of sales made, excluding sales tax

C   credited with the total purchases made, including sales tax

D   credited with the total expenses, excluding sales tax   (2 marks)

47   A business sold goods that had a net value of $600 to Lucid. What entries are required to record this transaction if sales tax is payable at 17.5%?

A   Dr Lucid $600, Dr Sales tax $105, Cr Sales $705

B   Dr Lucid $705, Cr Sales tax $105, Cr Sales $600

C   Dr Lucid $600, Cr Sales tax $105, Cr Sales $600

D   Dr Sales $600, Dr Sales tax $105, Cr Lucid $705   (2 marks)

48   Laker returned goods that had a net value of $200. What entries are required to record this transaction if sales tax is payable at 17.5%?

A   Dr Returns inward $200, Dr Sales tax $35, Cr Laker $235

B   Dr Returns inward $235, Cr Sales tax $35, Cr Laker $200

C   Dr Purchases $200, Dr Sales tax $35, Cr Laker $235

D   Dr Laker $235, Cr Returns inward $200, Cr Sales tax $35   (2 marks)

49 Stung, which is registered for the purposes of sales tax, bought furniture on credit terms at a cost of $8,000, plus tax of $1,200.

What is the correct account entry?

		$
A	Furniture	9,200
	Supplier	9,200
B	Furniture	8,000
	Sales tax	1,200
	Supplier	6,800
C	Furniture	8,000
	Sales tax	1,200
	Supplier	9,200
D	Furniture	8,000
	Supplier	8,000

(2 marks)

50 **Which of the following statements are true?**

1 Sales tax is a form of indirect taxation.

2 If input tax exceeds output tax the difference is payable to the authorities.

3 Sales tax is included in the reported sales and purchases of the business.

4 Sales tax cannot be recovered on some purchases.

A 1 and 4

B 1 and 2

C 2 and 3

D 3 and 4

(2 marks)

ACCRUALS AND PREPAYMENTS

51 **Leddley owns two properties which it rents to tenants. In the year ended 31 December 20X6, it received $280,000 in respect of property 1 and $160,000 in respect of property 2. Balances on the accrued income and prepaid expense accounts were as follows:**

	31 December 20X6	31 December 20X5
Property 1	13,400 Dr	12,300 Cr
Property 2	6,700 Cr	5,400 Dr

What amount should be credited to the statement of profit or loss for the year ended 31 December 20X6 in respect of rental income?

A $453,600

B $440,200

C $465,900

D $475,600

(2 marks)

52 Troy, a property company, received cash totalling $838,600 from tenants during the year ended 31 December 20X6.

Figures for rent in advance and in arrears at the beginning and end of the year were:

	31 December 20X5	31 December 20X6
	$	$
Rent received in advance	102,600	88,700
Rent in arrears (all subsequently received)	42,300	48,400

What amount should appear in the company's statement of profit or loss for the year ended 31 December 20X6 for rental income?

A $818,600

B $738,000

C $939,200

D $858,600   **(2 marks)**

53 **Details of Bartlett's insurance policy are shown below:**

Premium for year ended 31 March 20X6 paid April 20X5	$10,800
Premium for year ending 31 March 20X7 paid April 20X6	$12,000

What figures should be included in the company's financial statements for the year ended 30 June 20X6?

	Statement of profit or loss	Statement of financial position
	$	$
A	11,100	9,000 prepayment
B	11,700	9,000 prepayment
C	11,100	9,000 accrual
D	11,700	9,000 accrual

(2 marks)

54 **Vine sublets part of its office accommodation.**

The rent is received quarterly in advance on 1 January, 1 April, 1 July and 1 October. The annual rent has been $24,000 for some years, but it was increased to $30,000 from 1 July 20X5.

What amounts for rent should appear in the company's financial statements for the year ended 31 January 20X6?

	Profit or loss	Statement of financial position
A	$27,500	$5,000 in accrued income
B	$27,000	$2,500 in accrued income
C	$27,000	$2,500 in prepaid income
D	$27,500	$5,000 in prepaid income

(2 marks)

55   At 1 September, the motor expenses account showed 4 months' insurance prepaid of $80 and petrol accrued of $95. During September, the outstanding petrol bill is paid, plus further bills of $245. At 30 September there is a further outstanding petrol bill of $120.

The amount to be shown in the statement of profit or loss for motor expenses for September is:

A $385

B $415

C $445

D $460   (2 marks)

56   On 1 May 20X0, A pays a rent bill of $1,800 for the period to 30 April 20X1. What is the charge to the statement of profit or loss and the entry in the statement of financial position for the year ended 30 November 20X0?

A $1,050 charge to statement of profit or loss and prepayment of $750 in the statement of financial position

B $1,050 charge to statement of profit or loss and accrual of $750 in the statement of financial position

C $1,800 charge to statement of profit or loss and no entry in the statement of financial position

D $750 charge to statement of profit or loss and prepayment of $1,050 in the statement of financial position   (2 marks)

57   The electricity account for the year ended 30 June 20X3 was as follows:

	$
Opening balance for electricity accrued at 1 July 20X2	300
Payments made during the year:	
1 August 20X2 for three months to 31 July 20X2	600
1 November 20X2 for three months to 31 October 20X2	720
1 February 20X3 for three months to 31 January 20X3	900
30 June 20X3 for three months to 30 April 20X3	840

Which of the following is the appropriate entry for electricity?

	Accrued at June 20X3	Charged to statement of profit or loss, year ended 30 June 20X3
A	$Nil	$3,060
B	$460	$3,320
C	$560	$3,320
D	$560	$3,420 (2 marks)

58   The annual insurance premium for S for the period 1 July 20X3 to 30 June 20X4 is $13,200, which is 10% more than the previous year. Insurance premiums are paid on 1 July.

What is the statement of profit or loss charge for insurance for the year ended 31 December 20X3?

A $11,800

B $12,540

C $12,600

D $13,200   (2 marks)

59   Farthing's year-end is 30 September. On 1 January 20X6 the organisation took out a loan of $100,000 with annual interest of 12%. The interest is payable in equal instalments on the first day of April, July, October and January in arrears.

How much should be charged to the statement of profit or loss account for the year ended 30 September 20X6, and how much should be accrued on the statement of financial position?

	Statement of profit or loss	Statement of financial position
A	$12,000	$3,000
B	$9,000	$3,000
C	$9,000	Nil
D	$6,000	$3,000

(2 marks)

60   On the first day of Month 1, a business had prepaid insurance of $10,000. On the first day of Month 8, it paid, in full, the annual insurance invoice of $36,000, to cover the following year.

The amount charged in the statement of profit or loss and the amount shown in the statement of financial position at the year-end is:

	Statement of profit or loss	Statement of financial position
	$	$
A	5,000	24,000
B	22,000	23,000
C	25,000	21,000
D	36,000	15,000

(2 marks)

61   Which of the following statements is not true?

A   Accruals decrease profit

B   Accrued income decreases profit

C   A prepayment is an asset

D   A accrual is a liability   (2 marks)

IRRECOVERABLE DEBTS AND ALLOWANCES FOR RECEIVABLES

62   The following balances relate to Putney:

	$
Receivables at 1.1.X8	34,500
Cash received from credit customers	229,900
Contra with payables	1,200
Discounts allowed	17,890
Cash sales	24,000
Irrecoverable debts	18,600
Increase in allowance for receivables	12,500
Discounts received	15,670
Receivables at 31.12.X8	45,000

What is the revenue figure reported by Putney in the year ended 31 December 20X8?

A $275,870

B $278,090

C $290,590

D $302,090   (2 marks)

63   The following account has been extracted from the nominal ledger of Purdey:

Receivables ledger control account

	$		$
Balance b/f	84,700		
Contra with payables ledger control account	5,000	Irrecoverable debts	4,300
Discounts received	21,100	Discounts allowed	30,780
Credit sales	644,000	Cash received from credit customers	595,000
Cash sales	13,500	Increase in allowance for receivables	6,555
		Balance c/f	131,665
	768,300		768,300

After corrections, what is the receivables balance?

A $103,300

B $93,620

C $103,620

D $87,065   (2 marks)

64   Newell's receivables ledger control account shows a balance at the end of the year of $58,200 before making the following adjustments:

(i)   Newell wishes to write off debts amounting to $8,900 as he believes they are irrecoverable.

(ii)   He also wishes to make specific allowance for Carroll's debt of $1,350 and Juff's debt of $750.

(iii)   He wishes to maintain a general allowance of 3% of the year end receivables balance.

Newell's allowance for receivables at the last year end was $5,650.

What is the charge to the statement of profit or loss in respect of the above?

A $6,766

B $11,034

C $6,829

D $10,971   (2 marks)

65   In the statement of financial position at 31 December 20X5, Boris reported net receivables of $12,000. During 20X6 he made sales on credit of $125,000 and received cash from credit customers amounting to $115,500. At 31 December 20X6, Boris wished to write off debts of $7,100 and increase the allowance for receivables by $950 to $2,100. What is the net receivables figure at 31 December 20X6?

A $12,300

B $13,450

C $14,400

D $15,550   (2 marks)

66   At 1 July 20X5, a company's allowance for receivables was $48,000.

At 30 June 20X6, trade receivables amounted to $838,000. It was decided to write off $72,000 of these debts and adjust the allowance for receivables to $60,000.

What are the final amounts for inclusion in the company's statement of financial position at 30 June 20X6?

	Trade receivables	Allowance for receivables	Net balance
	$	$	$
A	838,000	60,000	778,000
B	766,000	60,000	706,000
C	766,000	108,000	658,000
D	838,000	108,000	730,000

(2 marks)

67 In the year ended 30 September 20X8, Fauntleroy had sales of $7,000,000. Year end receivables amounted to 5% of annual sales. Fauntleroy wishes to maintain the allowance for receivables at 4% of receivables and as a result discovers that the allowance is 20% higher than at the previous year end.

During the year irrecoverable debts amounting to $3,200 were written off and debts amounting to $450 and previously written off were recovered.

What is the irrecoverable debt expense for the year?

A $5,083

B $5,550

C $5,583

D $16,750   **(2 marks)**

68 On 1 January 20X3 Tipton's trade receivables were $10,000. The following relates to the year ended 31 December 20X3:

	$
Credit sales	100,000
Cash receipts	90,000
Discounts allowed	800
Discounts received	700

Cash receipts include $1,000 in respect of a receivable previously written off.

On 31 December 20X3 receivables were:

A $20,200

B $19,300

C $20,800

D $20,700   **(2 marks)**

69 A company has been notified that a customer has been declared bankrupt. The company had previously provided for this doubtful debt. Which of the following is the correct double entry?

	Dr	Cr
A	Irrecoverable debts account	Receivables ledger control account
B	Receivables ledger control account	Irrecoverable debts account
C	Allowance for receivables	Receivables ledger control account
D	Receivables ledger control account	Allowance for receivables

(2 marks)

70 **Headington is owed $37,500 by its customers at the start, and $39,000 at the end, of its year ended 31 December 20X8.**

During the period, cash sales of $263,500 and credit sales of $357,500 were made, discounts allowed amounted to $15,750 and discounts received $21,400. Irrecoverable debts of $10,500 were written off and Headington wishes to retain its allowance for receivables at 5% of total receivables.

The cash received from receivables in the year totalled:

A $329,750

B $593,175

C $593,250

D $614,650   **(2 marks)**

71 **The sales revenue in a company was $2 million and its receivables were 5% of sales. The company wishes to have an allowance for receivables of 4% of receivables, which would make the allowance one-third higher than the current allowance.**

How will the profit for the period be affected by the change in allowance?

A   Profit will be reduced by $1,000

B   Profit will be increased by $1,000

C   Profit will be reduced by $1,333

D   Profit will be increased by $1,333   **(2 marks)**

72 **A company started the year with total receivables of $87,000 and an allowance for receivables of $2,500.**

During the year, two specific debts were written off, one for $800 and the other for $550. A debt of $350 that had been written off as irrecoverable in the previous year was paid during the year. At the year end, total receivables were $90,000 and the allowance for receivables was $2,300.

What is the charge to the statement of profit or loss for the year in respect of irrecoverable and doubtful debts?

A $800

B $1,000

C $1,150

D $1,550   **(2 marks)**

73 **An increase in the allowance for receivables results in:**

A   an increase in net current assets

B   a decrease in net current assets

C   An increase in sales

D   A decrease in drawings   **(2 marks)**

74 At the end of 20X7, Chester's receivable's balance is $230,000. He wishes to make specific allowance for Emily's debt of $450 and Lulu's debt of $980. He also wishes to maintain a general allowance of 5% of receivables.

What amount should be charged or credited to the statement of profit or loss in respect of the allowance if the allowance at the start of the year was $11,700?

A $1,159 Dr

B $1,230 Dr

C $200 Cr

D $12,930 Dr   (2 marks)

75 Which of the following is not a benefit of providing credit to customers?

A   May result in increased sales

B   Encourages customer loyalty

C   Attracts new customers

D   Improves the cash flow of the business   (2 marks)

76 Which of the following best explains the purpose of an aged receivables analysis?

A   To ensure that credit is not extended to unapproved customers or those that in the past have not paid

B   To ensure that credit does not exceed agreed limits

C   To keep track of outstanding debts and follow up those that are overdue

D   To keep track of customer addresses   (2 marks)

NON-CURRENT ASSETS

77 The asset register shows a carrying value for non-current assets of $85,600; the ledger accounts include a cost balance of $185,000 and an accumulated depreciation balance of $55,000. Which of the following may explain the discrepancy?

A   The omission of an addition of land costing $30,000 from the ledger account and the omission of the disposal of an asset from the register (cost $25,600 and accumulated depreciation at disposal $11,200)

B   The omission of the revaluation of an asset upwards by $16,600 and the depreciation charge of $20,000 from the ledger account and the omission of the disposal of an asset with carrying value $41,000 from the register

C   The omission of the disposal of an asset from the ledger accounts (cost $25,600 and accumulated depreciation at disposal $11,200) and the omission of an addition of land costing $30,000 from the register.

D   The omission of an upwards revaluation by $16,400 from the register and the accidental debiting of the depreciation charge of $28,000 to the accumulated depreciation ledger account   (2 marks)

78   Laurie bought an asset on the 1st January 20X4 for $235,000. He has depreciated it at 30% using the reducing balance method. On 1st January 20X7, Laurie revalued the asset to $300,000.

What double entry should Laurie post to record the revaluation?

A   Dr Non-current assets cost $65,000   Cr Revaluation reserve $219,395

      Dr Accumulated depreciation $154,395

B   Dr Non-current assets cost $65,000   Cr Revaluation reserve $276,500

      Dr Accumulated depreciation $211,500

C   Dr Revaluation reserve $219,395   Cr Non-current assets cost $65,000

                                                                    Cr Accumulated depreciation $154,395

D   Dr Revaluation reserve $276,500   Cr Non-current assets cost $65,000

                                                                    Cr Accumulated depreciation $211,500

(2 marks)

79   **A non-current asset register is:**

A   an alternative name for the non-current asset ledger account

B   a list of the physical non-current assets rather than their financial cost

C   a schedule of planned maintenance of non-current assets for use by the plant engineer

D   a schedule of the cost and other information about each individual non-current asset

(2 marks)

80   **Which of the following four statements are correct?**

A   If all the conditions specified in IAS 38 Intangible assets are met, the directors can chose whether to capitalise the development expenditure or not.

B   Amortisation of capitalised development expenditure will appear as an item in a company's statement of changes in equity.

C   Capitalised development costs are shown in the statement of financial position as non-current assets.

D   Capitalised development expenditure must be amortised over a period not exceeding five years.   **(2 marks)**

81   The plant and equipment account in the records of a company for the year ended 31 December 20X6 is shown below:

Plant and equipment – cost

	$		$
Balance b/f	960,000		
1 July Cash	48,000	30 Sept Disposals	84,000
		Balance c/f	924,000
	1,008,000		1,008,000

The company's policy is to charge straight line depreciation at 20% per year on a pro rata basis.

What should be the charge for depreciation in the company's statement of profit or loss for the year ended 31 December 20X6?

A $184,800

B $192,600

C $191,400

D $184,200   (2 marks)

82   On 1 January 20X7, a company purchased some plant.

The invoice showed:

	$
Cost of plant	48,000
Delivery to factory	400
One year warranty covering breakdown	800
	49,200

Modifications to the factory building costing $2,200 were necessary to enable the plant to be installed.

What amount should be capitalised for the plant in the company's records?

A $51,400

B $48,000

C $50,600

D $48,400   (2 marks)

83   A non-current asset was purchased at the beginning of Year 1 for $2,400 and depreciated by 20% per annum using the reducing balance method. At the beginning of Year 4 it was sold for $1,200. The result of this was:

A   a loss on disposal of $240.00

B   a loss on disposal of $28.80

C   a profit on disposal of $28.80

D   a profit on disposal of $240.00   (2 marks)

PAPER F3 (FFA) : FINANCIAL ACCOUNTING

84 A business' non-current assets had a book value of $125,000. An asset which had cost $12,000 was sold for $9,000, at a profit of $2,000.

What is the revised book value of non-current assets?

A $113,000

B $118,000

C $125,000

D $127,000   (2 marks)

85 W bought a new printing machine from abroad. The cost of the machine was $80,000. The installation costs were $5,000 and the employees received specific training on how to use this particular machine, at a cost of $2,000. Before using the machine to print customers' orders, a test was undertaken which used up paper and ink costing $1,000.

What should be the cost of the machine in the company's statement of financial position?

A $80,000

B $85,000

C $86,000

D $88,000   (2 marks)

86 A non-current asset was disposed of for $2,200 during the last accounting year. It had been purchased exactly three years earlier for $5,000, with an expected residual value of $500, and had been depreciated on the reducing balance basis, at 20% per annum.

The profit or loss on disposal was:

A $360 loss

B $150 loss

C $104 loss

D $200 profit   (2 marks)

87 At the end of its financial year, Tanner has the following non-current assets:

Land and buildings at cost $10.4 million

Land and buildings: accumulated depreciation $0.12 million

The company has decided to revalue its land and buildings at the year end to $15 million.

What will be the amount of the adjustment on revaluation?

A $4.48m

B $4.6m

C $4.72m

D $15.12m   (2 marks)

88 **Which one of the following should be accounted for as capital expenditure?**

    A   The cost of painting a building

    B   The replacement of windows in a building

    C   The purchase of a car by a garage for re-sale

    D   Legal fees incurred on the purchase of a building   **(2 marks)**

89 **A car was purchased for $12,000 on 1 April 20X1 and has been depreciated at 20% each year straight line, assuming no residual value.**

The company policy is to charge a full year's depreciation in the year of purchase and no depreciation in the year of sale. The car was traded in for a replacement vehicle on 1 August 20X4 for an agreed figure of $5,000.

What was the profit or loss on the disposal of the vehicle for the year ended 31 December 20X4?

    A   Loss $2,200

    B   Loss $1,400

    C   Loss $200

    D   Profit $200   **(2 marks)**

90 **At 30 September 20X2, the following balances existed in the records of Lambda:**

Plant and equipment:

Cost	$860,000
Accumulated depreciation	$397,000

During the year ended 30 September 20X3, plant with a written down value of $37,000 was sold for $49,000. The plant had originally cost $80,000. Plant purchased during the year cost $180,000. It is the company's policy to charge a full year's depreciation in the year of acquisition of an asset and none in the year of sale, using a rate of 10% on the straight line basis.

What is the carrying value that should appear in Lambda's statement of financial position at 30 September 20X3 for plant and equipment?

    A $563,000

    B $467,000

    C $510,000

    D $606,000   **(2 marks)**

91 **Depreciation is best described as:**

    A   a means of spreading the payment for non-current assets over a period of years

    B   a decline in the market value of the assets

    C   a means of spreading the net cost of non-current assets over their estimated useful life

    D   a means of estimating the amount of money needed to replace the assets   **(2 marks)**

92 On 1 January 20X8, Wootton has a building in its books at cost $380,000, carrying value $260,000.

On 1 July 20X8, the asset is revalued at $450,000 and Wootton wishes to include that valuation in its books. Wootton's accounting policy is to depreciate buildings at 3% straight line.

The depreciation charge to the statement of profit or loss for the year ended 31 Dec is:

A $8,300

B $11,400

C $12,450

D $13,500   (2 marks)

93 A car was purchased by a newsagent business in May 20X1 for:

	$
Cost	10,000
Road tax	150
Total	10,150

The business adopts a date of 31 December as its year end.

The car was traded in for a replacement vehicle in August 20X5 at an agreed value of $5,000.

It has been depreciated at 25 per cent per annum on the reducing-balance method, charging a full year's depreciation in the year of purchase and none in the year of sale.

What was the profit or loss on disposal of the vehicle during the year ended December 20X5?

A   Profit: $718

B   Profit: $781

C   Profit: $1,788

D   Profit: $1,836   (2 marks)

94 The reducing balance method of depreciating non-current assets is more appropriate than the straight-line method when:

A   there is no expected residual value for the asset

B   the expected life of the asset is not capable of being estimated

C   the asset is expected to be replaced in a short period of time

D   the asset decreases in value less in later years than in the early years of use   (2 marks)

95   SSG bought a machine for $40,000 in January 20X1. The machine had an expected useful life of six years and an expected residual value of $10,000. The machine was depreciated on the straight-line basis. At the end of December 20X4, the machine was sold for $15,000. SSG charges pro rata depreciation.

The total amount charged to the statement of profit or loss over the life of the machine was:

A $15,000

B $20,000

C $25,000

D $30,000   (2 marks)

96   Liza bought a guillotine for her framing business for $20,000 on 1 July 20X7. She expected the guillotine to have a useful life of ten years and a residual value of $500.

On 1 July 20X8, Liza revises these estimations and believes the guillotine to have a remaining useful life of 5 years and no residual value.

What is the depreciation charge for the year ended 30 June 20X9?

A $3,220

B $3,610

C $4,000

D $3,600   (2 marks)

FROM TRIAL BALANCE TO FINANCIAL STATEMENTS

97   **Lord has extracted the following balances from his accounts:**

	$
Plant and machinery	89,000
Property	120,000
Inventory	4,600
Payables	6,300
Receivables	5,900
Bank overdraft	790
Loan	50,000
Capital	100,000
Drawings	23,000
Sales	330,000
Purchases	165,000
Sales returns	7,000
Discounts allowed	3,200
Discounts received	?
Sundry expenses	73,890

He has forgotten to extract the balance from the discounts received account. What is the balance?

A $1,900

B $9,500

C $4,500

D $15,900   (2 marks)

98 **Which of the following statements are true?**

1   The trial balance provides a check that no errors exist in the accounting records of a business.

2   The trial balance is a first step in the preparation of the financial statements.

A   1 only

B   2 only

C   Both 1 and 2

D   Neither 1 nor 2   **(2 marks)**

99 **Which of the following are limitations of the trial balance?**

1   It does not include final figures to be included in the financial statements.

2   It does not identify errors of commission.

3   It does not identify in what accounts errors have been made.

A   1 and 2

B   2 and 3 only

C   All 3

D   None of the above   **(2 marks)**

100 **The following is an extract from the trial balance of Gardeners:**

	Dr	Cr
	$	$
Non-current assets	50,000	
Inventory	2,600	
Capital		28,000
Receivables	4,500	
Allowance for receivables		320
Cash	290	
Payables		5,000
Sales		120,000
Purchases	78,900	
Rental expense	3,400	
Sundry expenses	13,900	
Bank interest		270
	———	———
	153,590	153,590
	———	———

- Rent of $200 has been prepaid.

- Inventory at the end of the year was $1,900.

- The allowance for receivables is to be $200.

What is the profit for the year?

A $23,690

B $23,610

C $23,100

D $25,500   **(2 marks)**

101 The following is an extract from the trial balance of Ardbark, a company. After making corrections, what is the revised balance on the suspense account?

	Dr	Cr
	$	$
Premises	500,000	
Accumulated depreciation		120,000
Inventory		23,000
Share capital	200,000	
Retained profits		105,000
Receivables	43,500	
Carriage in		1,500
Allowance for receivables		3,400
Bank overdraft	1,010	
Payables		35,900
Sales		500,080
Purchases	359,700	
Sales returns	10,300	
Sundry expenses	14,000	
Discounts allowed		1,340
Suspense		338,290
	1,128,510	1,128,510

A $15,710 Dr

B $14,730 Dr

C $12,050 Dr

D $33,630 Dr   **(2 marks)**

102 **The following year end adjustments are required:**

- Closing inventory of $45,700 to be recorded.

- Depreciation at 20% straight line to be charged on assets with a cost of $470,800.

- An Irrecoverable debt of $230 to be written off.

- Deferred income of $6,700 to be recorded.

What is the impact on net assets of these adjustments?

A $55,390 increase

B $55,390 decrease

C $41,990 decrease

D $41,990 increase   **(2 marks)**

103   **The following is the extract of Jordan's trial balance as at 31 December 20X7:**

	DR	CR
	$	$
Rent	22,000	
Insurance	30,000	

The following notes have been provided:

(i)   The monthly rent charge is $2,000.

(ii)   The annual insurance charge for the above year is $28,000.

What is the charge for rent and insurance for the year and the closing accrual and prepayment?

		Charge for the year		Closing
		$		$
A	Rent	22,000	Rent prepayment	2,000
	Insurance	28,000	Insurance prepayment	2,000
B	Rent	22,000	Rent accrual	2,000
	Insurance	30,000	Insurance prepayment	2,000
C	Rent	24,000	Rent accrual	2,000
	Insurance	28,000	Insurance prepayment	2,000
D	Rent	24,000	Rent accrual	2,000
	Insurance	30,000	Insurance accrual	2,000

(2 marks)

104   **The following is the extract of Jim's trial balance as at 31 December 20X7:**

	DR	CR
	$	$
Receivables	29,600	
Allowance for receivables		3,100
Irrecoverable debts	1,600	

The following notes are provided.

(i)   Additional irrecoverable debts of $3,000 were discovered at the year end.

(ii)   It has been decided to make an allowance for receivables of 10% on the adjusted receivables at the year end.

The total irrecoverable debts expense (irrecoverable debts and allowances for receivables) for the year ended 31 December 20X7 and the closing net receivables balance as at 31 December 20X7 will be:

	Irrecoverable debts expense	Net receivables
	$	$
A	4,160	23,940
B	5,040	23,940
C	2,560	21,830
D	4,000	19,800

(2 marks)

105   The following is the extract of Jenny's trial balance as at 31 December 20X7:

The policy of the business is to charge depreciation at 10% per annum on a straight line basis.

	DR	CR
	$	$
Plant and machinery	50,000	
Plant and machinery accumulated depreciation		15,000

What is the depreciation charge to the statement of profit or loss for the year ended 31 December 20X7 and the closing carrying value as at 31 December 20X7

	Depreciation charge	Carrying value
	$	$
A	3,500	31,500
B	5,000	30,000
C	5,000	45,000
D	3,500	30,000

(2 marks)

106   The following is the extract of Julian's trial balance as at 31 December 20X7:

	DR	CR
	$	$
Motor vehicles	50,000	
Motor vehicles accumulated depreciation		21,875

The policy of the business is to charge depreciation at 25% per annum on a reducing balance basis.

What is the statement of profit or loss depreciation charge for the year ended 31 December 20X7 and the closing carrying value as at 31 December 20X7?

Calculations to be rounded to the nearest $.

	Depreciation charge	Carrying value
	$	$
A	12,500	15,625
B	7,031	42,969
C	12,500	37,500
D	7,031	21,094

(2 marks)

BOOKS OF PRIME ENTRY AND CONTROL ACCOUNTS

107 **Which of the following are books of prime entry?**

A   Sales day book and trial balance

B   Petty cash book and accounts receivables ledger

C   Petty cash book and journal

D   Purchase day book and account payable ledger   **(2 marks)**

108 **The petty cash balance at 30 November 20X9 was $25. The following transactions occurred during the month:**

1   Biscuits were purchased at a cost of $7.25.

2   Travel expenses of $12.75 were reimbursed to an employee.

3   The cleaner was paid $15.

What is the imprest amount?

A $25

B $60

C $35

D $50   **(2 marks)**

109 **Which of the following explains the imprest system of operating petty cash?**

A   Weekly expenditure cannot exceed a set amount

B   The exact amount of expenditure is reimbursed at intervals to maintain a fixed float

C   All expenditure out of the petty cash must be properly authorised

D   Regular equal amounts of cash are transferred into petty cash at intervals   **(2 marks)**

110 **You are given the following figures for sales and receivables:**

	20X7	20X6
	$	$
Receivables at year end	74,963	69,472
Sales	697,104	
Total cash received from customers	686,912	
General allowance for receivables	750	695
Specific allowance for receivables	1,264	
Irrecoverable debts written off	1,697	

What was the value of sales returns during 20X7?

A $1,740

B $2,949

C $3,004

D $4,268   **(2 marks)**

111 Ignacius operates the imprest system for petty cash. At 1 July there was a float of $150, but it was decided to increase this to $200 from 1 August onwards. During July, the petty cashier received $25 from staff for using the photocopier and a cheque for $90 was cashed for an employee. In July, cheques were drawn for $500 for petty cash.

How much cash was paid out as cash expenses by the petty cashier in July?

A $385

B $435

C $515

D $615   **(2 marks)**

112 Which ONE of the following might explain a debit balance on a payables ledger account?

A   The company took a cash discount to which it was not entitled and paid less than the amount due

B   The company mistakenly paid too much

C   The book-keeper failed to enter a contra with the receivables ledger

D   The book-keeper failed to post a cheque paid to the account   **(2 marks)**

113 Allister's payables ledger control account has a balance at 1 October 20X8 of $34,500 credit.

During October, credit purchases were $78,400, cash purchases were $2,400 and payments made to suppliers, excluding cash purchases, and after deducting cash discounts of $1,200, were $68,900. Purchase returns were $4,700.

The closing balance was:

A $38,100

B $40,500

C $47,500

D $49,900   **(2 marks)**

114 The entries in a receivables ledger control account are:

Sales	$250,000
Bank	$225,000
Returns	$2,500
Irrecoverable debts	$3,000
Returned unpaid cheque	$3,500
Contra payables ledger account	$4,000

What is the balance on the receivables ledger control account?

A $12,000

B $19,000

C $25,000

D $27,000   **(2 marks)**

115 Which of the following is not the purpose of a receivables ledger control account?

A To provide a check on the arithmetic accuracy of the personal ledger

B To help to locate errors in the trial balance

C To ensure that there are no errors in the personal ledger

D To see the balance of total receivables at the end of a period **(2 marks)**

116 A credit entry of $450 on X's account in the books of Y could have arisen by:

A X buying goods on credit from Y

B Y paying X $450

C Y returning goods to X

D X returning goods to Y **(2 marks)**

117 Which of the following best describes the entries that are made using the sales day book totals at the end of each month?

A Debit sales with total net sales, credit receivables ledger control with total gross sales and credit sales tax account with total sales tax

B Debit sales with total gross sales, credit receivables ledger control with total net sales and credit sales tax account with total sales tax

C Debit receivables ledger control with total net sales, debit sales tax account with total sales tax and credit sales with total gross sales

D Debit receivables ledger control with total gross sales, credit sales with total net sales and credit sales tax account with total sales tax **(2 marks)**

118 A business' petty cash operates on an imprest system with an imprest of $100. All claims for payment must be supported by a third party voucher such as a receipt. Which of the following is the most cost-effective control that should be implemented in addition to the imprest?

A A designated petty cash cashier

B The petty cash tin kept in a locked drawer in a supervisor's office

C The imprest should be kept in a safe rather than a locked box

D Claims should be counter-signed by a manager **(2 marks)**

119 Which of the following best describes the purpose of a purchase invoice?

A Issued by a supplier as a request for payment

B Sent to supplier as a request for a supply

C Issued by supplier listing details of recent transactions

D Sent to the supplier as notification of payment **(2 marks)**

120 **Which of the following are documents issued by the customer in a transaction rather than the supplier?**

A   Quotation, goods delivery note and debit note

B   Goods delivery note, remittance advice and sales order

C   Purchase order and debit note

D   Sales order, purchase invoice and remittance advice   **(2 marks)**

CONTROL ACCOUNT RECONCILIATIONS

121 **A payables ledger control account showed a credit balance of $768,420. The payables ledger totalled $781,200.**

Which one of the following possible errors could account in full for the difference?

A   A contra against a receivables ledger debit balance of $6,390 has been entered on the credit side of the payables ledger control account

B   The total of discounts allowed $28,400 was entered to the debit side of the payables ledger control account instead of the correct figure for discounts received of $15,620

C $12,780 cash paid to a supplier was entered on the credit side of the supplier's account on the payables ledger

D   The total of discounts received $6,390 has been entered on the credit side of the payables ledger control account   **(2 marks)**

122 **The payables ledger control account below contains a number of errors:**

Payables ledger control account

	$		$
Balance b/f	318,600		
Cash paid to suppliers	1,364,300	Purchases	1,268,600
Purchase returns	41,200	Contras against debit balances in receivables ledger	48,000
Refunds received from suppliers	2,700	Discounts received	8,200
		Balance c/f	402,000
	1,726,800		1,726,800

All items relate to credit purchases.

What should be the closing balance when all the errors are corrected?

A $128,200

B $509,000

C $224,200

D $144,600   **(2 marks)**

123 Ordan received a statement from one of its suppliers, Alta, showing a balance due of $3,980. the amount due according to the payables ledger account of Ordan was only $230.

Comparison of the statement and the ledger account revealed the following differences:

1 A cheque sent by Ordan for $270 has not been recorded in Alta's statement.

2 Alta has not recorded goods returned by Ordan $180.

3 Ordan made a contra entry, reducing the amount due to Alta by $3,200, for a balance due from Alta in Ordan's receivables ledger. No such entry has been made in Alta's records.

What difference remains between the two companies' records after adjusting for these items?

A $460

B $640

C $6,500

D $100 **(2 marks)**

124 **A business' receivables ledger control account did not agree with the total of the balances on the receivables ledger. An investigation revealed that the sales day book had been overcast by $10. What effect will this have on the discrepancy?**

A The control account should be credited with $10

B The control account should be debited with $10

C The control account should be credited with $20

D The control account should be debited with $20 **(2 marks)**

125 **A supplier sends Lord a statement showing a balance outstanding of $14,350. Lord's records show a balance outstanding of $14,500.**

The reason for this difference could be that:

A the supplier sent an invoice for $150 which you have not yet received

B the supplier has allowed you $150 cash discount which you had omitted to enter in your ledgers

C you have paid the supplier $150 which he has not yet accounted for

D you have returned goods worth $150 which the supplier has not yet accounted for

(2 marks)

126 **Which of the following would NOT lead to a difference between the total of the balances on the receivables ledger and the balance on the receivables ledger control account?**

A An error in totalling the sales day book C/A

B An error in totalling the receipts column of the cash book C/A

C An overstatement of an entry in a customer's account LB

D An entry posted to the wrong customer's account LB **(2 marks)**

127 A receivables ledger control account showed a debit balance of $37,642. The individual customers' accounts in the receivables ledger showed a total of $35,840. The difference could be due to:

A undercasting the sales day book by $1,802

B overcasting the sales returns day book by $1,802

C entering a cash receipt of $1,802 on the debit side of a customer's account

D entering a cash discount allowed of $901 on the debit side of the control account

(2 marks)

128 Tarbuck has received a statement of account from one of its suppliers, showing an outstanding balance due to them of $1,350. On comparison with the ledger account, the following is determined:

- The ledger account shows a credit balance of $260.

- The supplier has disallowed a cash discount of $80 due to late payment of an invoice.

- The supplier has not yet allowed for goods returned at the end of the period of $270.

- Cash in transit of $830 has not been received by the supplier.

Following consideration of these items, the unreconciled difference between the two records is:

A $70

B $90

C $430

D $590

(2 marks)

129 The purchase day book of Arbroath has been undercast by $500, and the sales day book has been overcast by $700. Arbroath maintains payables and receivables ledger control accounts as part of the double entry bookkeeping system.

The effect of correcting these errors will be to:

A make adjustments to the ledger balances of the individual customers and suppliers, with no effect on profit

B make adjustments to the ledger balances of the individual customers and suppliers, with a decrease in profit of $1,200

C make adjustments to the control accounts, with no effect on profit

D make adjustments to the control accounts, with a decrease in profit of $1,200

(2 marks)

130   For the month of November 20X0 Figgin's purchases totalled $225,600 with sales tax of $33,840. The total of $259,440 has been credited to the payables ledger control account as $254,940.

Which of the following adjustments is correct?

	Control account	List of suppliers' balances
A	$4,500 Cr	No adjustment
B	$4,500 Cr	Increase by $4,500
C	$29,340 Dr	No effect
D	$33,840 Dr	Increase by $4,500

(2 marks)

131   In reconciling the receivables ledger control account with the list of receivables ledger balances of SK, the following errors were found:

1   The sales day book had been overcast by $370.

2   A total of $940 from the cash receipts book had been recorded in the receivables ledger control account as $490.

What adjustments must be made to correct the errors?

A   Credit sales control account $820. Decrease total of receivables ledger balances by $820

B   Credit sales control account $820. No change in total of receivables ledger balances.

C   Debit sales control account $80. No change in total of receivables ledger balances

D   Debit sales control account $80. Increase total of receivables ledger balances by $80

(2 marks)

BANK RECONCILIATIONS

132   The cash book of Worcester shows a credit balance of $1,350. Cheques of $56 have been written to suppliers but not yet cleared the bank; uncleared lodgements amount to $128. The bank has accidentally credited Worcester's account with interest of $15 due to another customer. A standing order of $300 has not been accounted for in the general ledger. What is the balance on the bank statement?

A $993 Cr

B $993 Dr

C $1,707 Cr

D $1,707 Dr

(2 marks)

133   Jo's bank ledger account shows a balance of $190 credit. Her bank statement reports a balance of $250 credit.

Which of the following will explain the difference in full?

A   Unpresented cheques of $100 and an uncleared lodgement of $30

B   Unpresented cheques of $150, the misposting of a cash receipt of $130 to the wrong side of the cash account and unrecorded bank interest received of $30

C   An unrecorded direct debit of $30, a dishonoured cheque of $70 and an uncleared lodgement of $40

D   An unrecorded standing order of $60, an unpresented cheque of $110 and a bank error whereby Jo's account was accidentally credited with $110   **(2 marks)**

134   **Which of the following statements about bank reconciliations are correct?**

1   In preparing a bank reconciliation, unpresented cheques must be deducted from a balance of cash at bank shown in the bank statement.

2   A cheque from a customer paid into the bank but dishonoured must be corrected by making a debit entry in the cash book.

3   An error by the bank must be corrected by an entry in the cash book.

4   An overdraft is a debit balance in the bank statement.

A   1 and 3

B   2 and 3

C   1 and 4

D   2 and 4   **(2 marks)**

135   **The following bank reconciliation statement has been prepared by an inexperienced bookkeeper at 31 December 20X5:**

	$
Balance per bank statement (overdrawn)	(38,640)
Add: Lodgements not credited	19,270
	57,010
Less: Unpresented cheques	(14,260)
Balance per cash book	43,650

What should the final cash book balance be when all the above items have been properly dealt with?

A $43,650 overdrawn

B $33,630 overdrawn

C $5,110 overdrawn

D $72,170 overdrawn   **(2 marks)**

136 A bank reconciliation statement for Dallas at 30 June 20X5 is being prepared. The following information is available:

1   Bank charges of $2,340 have not been entered in the cash book.

2   The bank statement shows a balance of $200 Dr.

3   Unpresented cheques amount to $1,250.

4   A direct debit of $250 has not been recorded in the ledger accounts.

5   A bank error has resulted in a cheque for $97 being debited to Dallas' account instead of Dynasty's account.

6   Cheques received but not yet banked amounted to $890.

The final balance in the cash book after all necessary adjustments should be

A $463 Dr

B $463 Cr

C $63 Cr

D $63 Dr   **(2 marks)**

137 The following information relates to a bank reconciliation.

1   The bank balance in the cash book before taking the items below into account was $8,970 overdrawn.

2   Bank charges of $550 on the bank statement have not been entered in the cash book.

3   The bank has credited the account in error with $425 which belongs to another customer.

4   Cheque payments totalling $3,275 have been entered in the cashbook but have not been presented for payment.

5   Cheques totalling $5,380 have been correctly entered on the debit side of the cashbook but have not been paid in at the bank.

What was the balance as shown by the bank statement before taking the items above into account?

A $8,970 overdrawn

B $11,200 overdrawn

C $12,050 overdrawn

D $17,750 overdrawn   **(2 marks)**

138   Sharmin's bank statement at 31 October 20X8 shows a balance of $13,400. She subsequently discovers that the bank has dishonoured a customer's cheque for $300 and has charged bank charges of $50, neither of which is recorded in the cash book.

There are unpresented cheques totalling $1,400 and an automatic receipt from a customer of $195 has been recorded as a credit in Sharmin's cash book.

Sharmin's cash book balance, prior to correcting the errors and omissions, was:

   A $11,455

   B $11,960

   C $12,000

   D $12,155   (2 marks)

139   Wimborne's bank statement shows a balance of $715 overdrawn. The statement includes bank charges of $74 which have not been entered in the cash book. There are also unpresented cheques totalling $824 and lodgements not yet credited of $337. In addition the bank statement erroneously includes a dividend receipt of $25 belonging to another customer.

The bank overdraft in the statement of financial position should be:

   A $253

   B $1,177

   C $1,202

   D $1,227   (2 marks)

140   The cash book shows a bank balance of $5,675 overdrawn at 31 August 20X5. It is subsequently discovered that a standing order for $125 has been entered twice, and that a dishonoured cheque for $450 has been debited in the cash book instead of credited. The correct bank balance should be:

   A $5,100 overdrawn

   B $6,000 overdrawn

   C $6,250 overdrawn

   D $6,450 overdrawn   (2 marks)

141   An organisation's cash book has an opening balance of $485 credit. The following transactions then took place:

Cash sales $1,450 including sales tax of $150.

Receipts from customers of debts of $2,400.

Payments to suppliers of debts of $1,800 less 5% cash discount.

Dishonoured cheques from customers amounting to $250.

The resulting balance in the cash book should be:

   A $1,255 debit

   B $1,405 debit

   C $1,905 credit

   D $2,375 credit   (2 marks)

142   The bank statement at 31 October 20X7 showed an overdraft of $800. On reconciling the bank statement, it was discovered that a cheque drawn by your company for $80 had not been presented for payment, and that a cheque for $130 from a customer had been dishonoured on 30 October 20X7, but that this had not yet been notified to you by the bank.

The correct bank balance to be shown in the statement of financial position at 31 October 20X7 is:

A $1,010 overdrawn

B $880 overdrawn

C $750 overdrawn

D $720 overdrawn   (2 marks)

143   Your firm's cash book at 30 April 20X8 shows a balance at the bank of $2,490. Comparison with the bank statement at the same date reveals the following differences:

	$
Unpresented cheques	840
Bank charges not in cash book	50
Receipts not yet credited by the bank	470
Dishonoured cheque not in cash book	140

The correct bank balance at 30 April 20X8 is:

A $1,460

B $2,300

C $2,580

D $3,140   (2 marks)

144   Your firm's cash book shows a credit bank balance of $1,240 at 30 April 20X9. On comparison with the bank statement, you determine that there are unpresented cheques totalling $450, and a receipt of $140 which has not yet been passed through the bank account. The bank statement shows bank charges of $75 which have not been entered in the cash book.

The balance on the bank statement is:

A $1,005 overdrawn

B $930 overdrawn

C $1,475 in credit

D $1,550 in credit   (2 marks)

145   Which of the following is not an 'unrecorded difference' when reconciling the balance on the cash book to the amount shown in the bank statement?

A   A standing order

B   Bank interest

C   An uncleared lodgement

D   A BACS receipt   (2 marks)

CORRECTION OF ERRORS AND SUSPENSE ACCOUNTS

146 A trial balance shows a total of debits of $347,800 and a total of credits of $362,350.

After adjusting for the following errors, what is the balance on the suspense account?

(1) A credit sale of $3,670 was incorrectly entered in the sales day book as $3,760.

(2) A non-current asset with a carrying value of $7,890 was disposed of for $9,000. The only accounting entry was to debit cash.

(3) The allowance for receivables was increased from $8,900 to $10,200. The allowance account was debited in error.

A $26,150 debit

B $26,060 debit

C $26,240 debit

D $2,950 credit   (2 marks)

147 The trial balance of Kelvin does not balance. Which two of the following errors could explain this, assuming that Kelvin maintains control accounts for its receivables and payables within the double entry system?

(1) The sales day book was undercast by $100.

(2) Discounts allowed were debited to the discounts received account.

(3) An opening accrual was omitted from the rent account.

(4) The debit side of the cash account was undercast.

A   (1) and (2)

B   (2) and (3)

C   (3) and (4)

D   (1) and (4)   (2 marks)

148 The trial balance of MHSB does not balance at the year end. What type of error may explain this?

A   Extraction error

B   Error of commission

C   Compensating error

D   An error of principle   (2 marks)

149 The trial balance of Bob Butler shows total debts of $125,819 and total credits of $118,251. Which of the following explains the difference in full?

A   Discounts allowed of $3,784 have been shown on the wrong side of the trial balance

B   Discounts received of $3,784 have been credited to the payables ledger control account

C   The sales day book has been undercast by $7,568

D   An opening accrual of $7,568 has been omitted from the rental expense account

                                                                                    (2 marks)

150 **Which one of the following journals is correct according to its narrative?**

		Debit	Credit
		$	$
A	Mr Smith personal account	100,000	
	Directors' remuneration		100,000
	Bonus allocated to account of managing director (Mr Smith)		
B	Purchases	14,000	
	Wages	24,000	
	Repairs to buildings		38,000
	Transfer of costs of repairs to buildings carried out by company employees using materials from inventory		
C	Discounts allowed	2,800	
	Discounts received		2,800
	Correction of error: discounts allowed total incorrectly debited to discounts received account.		
D	Suspense account	20,000	
	Rent receivable		10,000
	Rent payable		10,000
	Correction of error: rent received credited in error to rent payable account.		

(2 marks)

151 **The trial balance of Koi did not balance, and a suspense account was opened for the difference.**

Which of the following errors would require an entry to the suspense account in correcting them?

1   A cash payment to purchase a motor van had been correctly entered in the cash book but had been debited to the motor expenses account.

2   The debit side of the wages account had been undercast.

3   The total of the discounts allowed column in the cash book had been posted to the receivables ledger control account correctly and credited to the discounts received account.

4   A cash refund to a customer had been recorded by debiting the cash book and crediting the customer's account.

A   1 and 2

B   2 and 3

C   3 and 4

D   2 and 4

(2 marks)

152 A company's trial balance failed to agree, and a suspense account was opened for the difference.

Subsequent checking revealed that discounts allowed of $13,000 had been credited to the discounts received account and an entry on the credit side of the cash book for the purchase of some machinery costing $18,000 had not been posted to the plant and machinery account.

Which two of the following journal entries would correct the errors?

		Debit $	Credit $
1	Discounts allowed	13,000	
	Discounts received		13,000
2	Discounts allowed	13,000	
	Discounts received	13,000	
	Suspense account		26,000
3	Suspense account	26,000	
	Discounts allowed		13,000
	Discounts received		13,000
4	Plant and machinery	18,000	
	Suspense account		18,000
5	Suspense account	18,000	
	Plant and machinery		18,000

A 1 and 4

B 2 and 5

C 2 and 4

D 3 and 5

(2 marks)

This information is relevant to the following TWO questions:

A company's draft financial statements for 20X5 showed a profit of $630,000. However, the trial balance did not agree, and a suspense account appeared in the company's financial statements.

Subsequent checking revealed the following errors:

1   The cost of an item of plant $48,000 had been entered in the cash book and in the plant account as $4,800. Depreciation at the rate of 10% per year ($480) had been charged.

2   Bank charges of $440 appeared in the bank statement in December 20X5 but had not been entered in the company's records.

3   One of the directors paid $800 due to a supplier in the company's payables ledger by a personal cheque. The bookkeeper recorded a debit in the supplier's ledger account but did not complete the double entry for the transaction (The company does not maintain a payables ledger control account).

4   The payments side of the cash book had been understated by $10,000.

153   **Which of the above items would require an entry to the suspense account in correcting them?**

    A   All four items

    B   3 and 4 only

    C   2 and 3 only

    D   1, 2 and 4 only   **(2 marks)**

154   **What would the company's profit become after the correction of the above errors?**

    A $634,760

    B $624,760

    C $624,440

    D $625,240   **(2 marks)**

155   **The draft accounts of Galahad's business for the year ended 31 July 20X0 show a profit of $54,250 prior to the correction of the following errors:**

    1   Cash drawings of $250 have not been accounted for.

    2   Debts amounting to $420, which were provided against in full during the year, should have been written off as irrecoverable.

    3   Rental income of $300 has been classified as interest receivable.

    4   On the last day of the accounting period, $200 in cash was received from a customer, but no bookkeeping entries have yet been made.

    What is the correct profit of the business for the year?

    A $53,580

    B $53,830

    C $54,250

    D $55,830   **(2 marks)**

156 The trial balance of Flo, a limited liability company, does not agree and a suspense account has been opened.

Inventory bought at a tax inclusive cost of $4,700 has been credited to the payables ledger control account. The sales tax, at 17.5%, has been recorded in the sales tax account and the total $4,700 has been recorded in the purchases account.

What entry is required to correct the error?

A   Dr Payables ledger control account $700   Cr Suspense account $700

B   Dr Payables ledger control account $822.50   Cr Suspense account $822.50

C   Dr Suspense account $700   Cr Purchases $700

D   Dr Suspense account $822.50   Cr Purchases $822.50   **(2 marks)**

157 **Weagan's trial balance at 31 October 20X9 is out of agreement, with the debit side totalling $500 less than the credit side. During November, the following errors are discovered:**

- The credit side of the sales account for October had been undercast by $150.

- Rent received of $240 had been credited to the rent payable account.

- The allowance for receivables, which decreased by $420, had been recorded in the allowance for receivables account as an increase.

Following the correction of these errors, the balance on the suspense account would be:

A $190 Cr

B $670 Cr

C $1,190 Cr

D $1,490 Dr   **(2 marks)**

158 **Which ONE of the following is an error of principle?**

A   A gas bill credited to the gas account and debited to the bank account

B   The purchase of a non-current asset credited to the asset at cost account and debited to the supplier's account

C   The purchase of a non-current asset debited to the purchases account and credited to the supplier's account

D   The payment of wages debited and credited to the correct accounts, but using the wrong amount   **(2 marks)**

159 **The trial balance of C did not agree, and a suspense account was opened for the difference. Checking in the bookkeeping system revealed a number of errors:**

Error

1   $4,600 paid for motor van repairs was correctly treated in the cash book but was credited to motor vehicles asset account.

2   $360 received from Brown, a customer, was credited in error to the account of Green.

3   $9,500 paid for rent was debited to the rent account as $5,900.

4   The total of the discount allowed column in the cash book had been debited in error to the discounts received account.

5   No entries had been made to record a cash sale of $100.

Which of the errors above would require an entry to the suspense account as part of the process of correcting them?

A   Errors 3 and 4 only

B   Errors 1 and 3 only

C   Errors 2 and 5 only

D   Errors 2 and 3 only   **(2 marks)**

160 **Drive gives a cash discount of $40 to a customer. The discount is credited to the discounts allowed account.**

The effect of recording the discount in this way is that profit will be:

A   correct

B   overstated by $80

C   understated by $80

D   understated by $40.   **(2 marks)**

161 **A suspense account was opened when a trial balance failed to agree. The following errors were later discovered:**

Error

1   A gas bill of $420 had been recorded in the Gas account as $240.

2   Discount of $50 given to a customer had been credited to Discounts Received.

3   Interest received of $70 had been entered in the bank account only.

The original balance on the suspense account was:

A   debit $210

B   credit $210

C   debit $160

D   credit $160   **(2 marks)**

162 The book-keeper of High Hurdles was instructed to make a contra entry for $270 between the supplier account and the customer account for Greyfold. He recorded the transaction by debiting the customer account and crediting the supplier account with $270. The business accounts do not include control accounts.

Which of the following statements is correct?

A   Unless the error is corrected, profit will be over-stated by $540

B   Unless the error is corrected, net assets will be over-stated by $270

C   Unless the error is corrected, net assets will be over-stated by $540

D   The errors should be corrected, but neither the profit nor the net assets are over-stated

(2 marks)

INCOMPLETE RECORDS

163 On 1 September 20X8, Winston had inventory of $380,000. During the month, sales totalled $650,000 and purchases $480,000. On 30 September 20X8 a fire destroyed some of the inventory. The undamaged goods were valued at $220,000. The business operates with a standard gross profit margin of 30%.

Based on this information, what is the cost of the inventory destroyed in the fire?

A $185,000

B $140,000

C $405,000

D $360,000

(2 marks)

164 The following information is available about the transactions of Razil, a sole trader who does not keep proper accounting records:

	$
Opening inventory	77,000
Closing inventory	84,000
Purchases	763,000
Gross profit margin	30%

Based on this information, what is Razil's sales revenue for the year?

A $982,800

B $1,090,000

C $2,520,000

D $1,080,000

(2 marks)

165 You are given the following incomplete and incorrect extract from the statement of profit or loss of a company that trades at a mark up of 25% on cost:

	$	$
Sales		174,258
Less: Cost of goods sold		
Opening inventory	12,274	
Purchases	136,527	
Closing inventory	X	
		(X)
Gross profit		X

Having discovered that the sales figure should have been $174,825 and that purchase returns of $1,084 and sales returns of $1,146 have been omitted, the closing inventory should be:

A $8,662

B $8,774

C $17,349

D $17,458   (2 marks)

166 A fire in the offices of Lewis has destroyed most of the accounting records.

The following information has been retrieved:

	$
Sales	630,000
Opening inventory	24,300
Closing inventory	32,750
Opening payables	29,780
Closing payables	34,600

Gross profit for the period should represent a mark up of 40%.

What was the total cash paid to suppliers in the year?

A $463,270

B $381,630

C $391,270

D $453,630   (2 marks)

167 Pioneer's annual inventory count took place on 6 January 20X6. The value of inventory on this date was $32,780. During the period from 31 December 20X5 to 6 January 20X6, the following events occurred:

Sales	$8,600
Purchases	$4,200

The value of inventory at 31 December 20X5 was $34,600.

What is the gross margin of Pioneer?

A   70%

B   72%

C   30%

D   43%   **(2 marks)**

168 Harry has a mark up of 25% on cost of sales. The following information is also available:

	$
Receivables at start of year	6,340
Receivables at end of year	5,200
Cash at start of year	620
Cash at end of year	500
Total cash payments	16,780

The only receipts during the year consisted of cash and cheques received from customers.

What is the gross profit for the year?

A $3,880

B $3,152

C $3,560

D $3,104   **(2 marks)**

169 During September, Edel had sales of $148,000, which made a gross profit of $40,000. Purchases amounted to $100,000 and opening inventory was $34,000.

The value of closing inventory was:

A $24,000

B $26,000

C $42,000

D $54,000   **(2 marks)**

170 The gross profit mark-up is 40% where:

A   sales are $120,000 and gross profit is $48,000

B   sales are $120,000 and cost of sales is $72,000

C   sales are $100,800 and cost of sales is $72,000

D   sales are $100,800 and cost of sales is $60,480   **(2 marks)**

171 From the following information, calculate the value of purchases:

	$
Opening trade payables	142,600
Cash paid	542,300
Discounts received	13,200
Goods returned	27,500
Closing trade payables	137,800

    A $302,600

    B $506,400

    C $523,200

    D $578,200   **(2 marks)**

172 You are given the following information:

Receivables at 1 January 20X3	$10,000
Receivables at 31 December 20X3	$9,000
Total receipts during 20X3 (including cash sales of $5,000)	$85,000

Sales during 20X3 amount to:

    A $81,000

    B $86,000

    C $79,000

    D $84,000   **(2 marks)**

173 P is a sole proprietor whose accounting records are incomplete. All the sales are cash sales and during the year $50,000 was banked, including $5,000 from the sale of a business car. He paid $12,000 wages in cash from the till and withdrew $2,000 per month as drawings. The cash in the till at the beginning and end of the year was $300 and $400 respectively.

What were the sales for the year?

    A $80,900

    B $81,000

    C $81,100

    D $86,100   **(2 marks)**

174   Many of the records of G have been destroyed by fire. The following information is available for the period under review.

(i)   Sales totalled $480,000.

(ii)   Inventory at cost was opening $36,420, closing $40,680.

(iii) Trade payables were opening $29,590, closing $33,875.

(iv)   Gross profit for the period should represent a mark-up on cost of 50%.

What was the total for the period of cash paid to suppliers?

A $239,975

B $315,715

C $319,975

D $328,545   (2 marks)

175   Pike runs an angling shop in the south of Spain. He spends all of his spare time fishing and consequently has kept no accounting records in the year ended 31 August 20X5. He knows that he has taken $6,800 cash out of his business during the year plus bait which cost the business $250. He can also remember putting his $20,000 winnings on the Spanish lottery into the business in March.

Pike knows that at the last year end his business had assets of $40,000 and liabilities of $14,600. He has also calculated that the assets of the business at 31 August 20X5 are worth $56,000, and the liabilities $18,750.

What profit or loss has Pike made in the year?

A $1,100 profit

B $1,100 loss

C $1,350 profit

D $1,350 loss   (2 marks)

176   Ives makes and sells handmade pottery. He keeps all finished items in a storeroom at the back of his workshop on the banks of the River Flow.   In August 20X5, freak weather conditions led to extensive flooding, and Ives lost pottery which had cost $3,400 and had a retail value of $5,750.

Ives was insured for loss of inventory due to flooding.

What double entry is required to record the loss of Inventory?

	Dr	Cr
A	Expense (IS) $5,750	Cost of sales (IS) $5,750
B	Current asset (SFP) $5,750	Cost of sales (IS) $5,750
C	Expense (IS) $3,400	Cost of sales (IS) $3,400
D	Current asset (SFP) $3,400	Cost of sales (IS) $3,400

(2 marks)

COMPANY ACCOUNTS

177   The following information is relevant to Wimbledon:

	$
Opening inventory	12,500
Closing inventory	17,900
Purchases	199,000
Distribution costs	35,600
Administrative expenses	78,800
Audit fee	15,200
Carriage in	3,500
Carriage out	7,700
Depreciation	40,000

Depreciation is to be split in the ratio 30:70 between the office and factory.

What is the cost of sales?

A $233,600

B $221,600

C $225,100

D $237,100   **(2 marks)**

178   Brown has $100,000 50c shares and $400,000 8% irredeemable preference shares in issue. A dividend of 3c per ordinary share and half of the preference dividend were paid during the year.

Which of the following statements are true?

1   An ordinary dividend of $3,000 is paid during the year.

2   A preference dividend of $16,000 is accrued at the year end.

A   1 only

B   2 only

C   Neither 1 nor 2

D   Both 1 and 2   **(2 marks)**

179   At 1 October 20X6, Ozber's capital was structured as follows:

	$
Ordinary shares of 25c	100,000
Share premium	30,000

On 10 January 20X7, in order to raise finance for expansion, there was a 1 for 4 rights issue at $1.15. The issue was fully taken up. This was followed by a 1 for 10 bonus issue on 1 June 20X7.

What is the balance on the share premium account after these transactions?

A $17,500

B $21,250

C $107,500

D $120,000   **(2 marks)**

180 Where in a company's financial statements complying with International accounting standards, should you find dividends paid?

1   Statement of profit or loss and other comprehensive income.

2   Statement of financial position.

3   Statement of cash flows.

4   Statement of changes in equity.

A   1 and 3

B   2 and 3

C   1 and 4

D   3 and 4   **(2 marks)**

181 Where in the financial statements should tax on profit for the current period, and unrealised surplus on revaluation of properties, be separately disclosed?

	Tax on profit for the current period	*Unrealised surplus on revaluation of properties*
A	Statement of profit or loss and other comprehensive income	Statement of cash flows
B	Statement of changes in equity	Statement of profit or loss and other comprehensive income
C	Statement of profit or loss and other comprehensive income	Statement of profit or loss and other comprehensive income
D	Statement of cash flows	Statement of cash flows

(2 marks)

182 The following information is available about a company's dividends:

Sept 20X5	Final dividend for the year ended 30 June 20X5 paid (declared August 20X5)	$100,000
March 20X6	Interim dividend for the year ended 30 June 20X6 paid	$40,000
Sept 20X6	Final dividend for the year ended 30 June 20X6 paid (declared August 20X6)	$120,000

What figures, if any, should be disclosed in the company's statement of profit or loss and other comprehensive income for the year ended 30 June 20X6 and its statement of financial position at that date?

	Statement of profit or loss and other comprehensive income	*Statement of financial position*
A	$160,000 deduction	$120,000
B	$140,000 deduction	Nil
C	Nil	$120,000
D	Nil	Nil

(2 marks)

183 **Which of the following statements are correct?**

1   A company might make a rights issue if it wished to raise more equity capital.

2   A rights issue might increase the share premium account whereas a bonus issue is likely to reduce it.

3   A rights issue will always increase the number of shareholders in a company whereas a bonus issue will not.

4   A bonus issue will result in the market value of each share increasing

A   1 and 2

B   1 and 3

C   2 and 3

D   2 and 4   **(2 marks)**

184 **Florabundi, a limited liability company, shows an overprovision of $3,400 on its tax liability account at the end of the year ended 31 December 20X8 before accounting for that year's tax charge.**

It estimates tax on profits for the year to be $67,900.

What amounts should be shown in the financial statements for the year ended 31 December 20X8 in respect of tax?

	Statement of profit or loss	Statement of financial position
A	$67,900 tax charge	$67,900 tax payable
B	$64,500 tax charge	$64,500 tax payable
C	$64,500 tax charge	$67,900 tax payable
D	$71,300 tax charge	$67,900 tax payable

(2 marks)

185 **Classify the following assets and liabilities as current or non-current in Albatross, a limited liability company's accounts:**

1   A sale has been made on credit to a customer. They have agreed to terms stating that payment is due in 12 months time.

2   A bank overdraft facility of $30,000 is available under an agreement with the bank which extends 2 years.

3   A company has bought a small number of shares in another company which it intends to trade.

4   A bank loan has been taken out with a repayment date 5 years hence.

	Current	Non-current
A	2 and 3	1 and 4
B	3 only	1, 2 and 4
C	1, 2 and 3	4
D	1 and 3	2 and 4

(2 marks)

186 Extracts from the accounting records of Andratx, a company, relating to the year ended 31 December 20X6 are as follows:

Revaluation surplus	$230,000
Ordinary interim dividend paid	$12,000
Profit before tax	$178,000
Estimated tax liability for year	$45,000
8% $1 Preference shares	$100,000
Under provision for tax in previous year	$5,600
Proceeds of issue of 2,000 $1 ordinary Shares	$5,000
Final ordinary dividend proposed	$30,000

What is the total change reported in the statement of changes in equity for the year?

A $312,400

B $356,000

C $348,000

D $342,400   (2 marks)

187 Which of the following statements are true of a preference share?

1   They carry voting rights.

2   Their dividend is paid out in priority to an ordinary dividend.

3   Their dividend is related to profits.

A   All 3

B   1 and 2

C   2 and 3

D   2 only   (2 marks)

188 Bangeroo, a company, issues 100,000 3% $1 redeemable preference shares during the year ended 30 September 20X8 at 98c per share. What is the correct entry to account for this transaction?

		Debit		Credit
		$		$
A	Cash	$98,000	Liability	$98,000
B	Cash	$98,000	Share capital	$100,000
	Share premium	$2,000		
C	Cash	$98,000	Share capital	$98,000
D	Cash	$98,000	Share capital	$100,000
	Statement of profit or loss	$2,000		

(2 marks)

189   The nominal value paid by the shareholder plus further amounts that they have agreed to pay in the future' best describes:

    A   Paid up share capital

    B   Called up share capital

    C   Authorised share capital

    D   Issued share capital   **(2 marks)**

190   Argonaut, a company, issues $400,000 12% loan notes for $380,000 on 1 August 20X6. What accounting entries are required in the year ended 30 September 20X6?

A	Dr Cash		$400,000
	Cr Non-current liabilities	$400,000	
	And		
	Dr Interest	$7,600	
	Cr Current liabilities	$7,600	
B	Dr Cash		$380,000
	Cr Non-current liabilities	$380,000	
	And		
	Dr Interest	$8,000	
	Cr Current liabilities	$8,000	
C	Dr Cash		$400,000
	Cr Non-current liabilities	$400,000	
	And		
	Dr Interest	$8,000	
	Cr Current liabilities	$8,000	
D	Dr Cash		$380,000
	Cr Non-current liabilities	$380,000	
	And		
	Dr Interest	$7,600	
	Cr Current liabilities	$7,600	**(2 marks)**

191   Which of the following are advantages of a bonus issue?

    1   It is the cheapest way for a company to raise finance through the issuing of shares.

    2   It makes the shares in the company more marketable.

    3   The total reserves of the business will increase.

    4   Issued share capital is brought more into line with assets employed in the company.

    A   2 and 4

    B   1 and 2

    C   3 and 4

    D   1 and 3   **(2 marks)**

192 **Revenue reserves would decrease if a company**

A   sets aside profits to pay future dividends

B   transfers amounts into 'general reserves'

C   issues shares at a premium

D   pays dividends

(2 marks)

ACCOUNTING STANDARDS

193 **Ribblesdale prepares its accounts to a 30 September year end. Its accounts for the year ended 30 September 20X8 are approved on 12 January 20X9 and issued on 20 February 20X9.**

Which of the following is an adjusting event after the reporting period?

A   A flood destroys inventory which cost $1,700 on 3 December 20X8.

B   A credit customer with an outstanding balance at the year end was declared bankrupt on 20 January 20X9.

C   Inventory valued at a cost of $800 in the year end accounts was sold for $650 on 11 January 20X9.

D   An ordinary dividend of 4c per share was declared on 1 December 20X8.   **(2 marks)**

194 **Which of the following requires a provision per IAS 37?**

1   A retail outlet has a policy of providing refunds over and above the statutory requirement to do so. This policy is well publicised.

2   A customer has made a legal claim against a company, claiming that faulty goods sold to them caused damage to their property. The company's lawyers have advised that the claim will possibly succeed.

A   1 only

B   2 only

C   1 and 2

D   Neither   **(2 marks)**

195 **Intangible assets are disclosed in the notes to the accounts at:**

A   Cost price

B   Cost – amortisation = CV

C   The amortisation amount

D   At the disposal proceeds value   **(2 marks)**

196 **An intangible asset is:**

A   an asset with no physical substance

B   an asset generated internally by a business

C   a purchased asset which has no physical substance

D   an asset which cannot be used to generate profits in the business   **(2 marks)**

197 **Which of the following statements about the requirements of IAS 37 *Provisions, Contingent Liabilities and Contingent Assets* are correct?**

1   A contingent asset should be disclosed by note if an inflow of economic benefits is probable.

2   No disclosure of a contingent liability is required if the possibility of a transfer of economic benefits arising is remote.

3   Contingent assets must not be recognised in financial statements unless an inflow of economic benefits is virtually certain to arise.

A   All three statements are correct

B   1 and 2 only

C   1 and 3 only

D   2 and 3 only   **(2 marks)**

198 **Which of the following statements are correct according to IAS 10 *Events After the Reporting Period*?**

1   Details of all adjusting events must be disclosed by note to the financial statements.

2   A material loss arising from the sale, after the reporting date of inventory valued at cost at the statement of financial position date must be reflected in the financial statements.

3   If the market value of investments falls materially after the reporting date, the details must be disclosed by note.

4   Events after the reporting date are those that occur between the statement of financial position date and the date when the financial statements are approved.

A   1 and 2 only

B   1, 3 and 4

C   2 and 3 only

D   2, 3 and 4   **(2 marks)**

199 **The following items have to be considered in finalising the financial statements of Quidditch, a limited liability company:**

1   The company gives warranties on its products. The company's statistics show that about 5% of sales give rise to a warranty claim.

2   The company has guaranteed the overdraft of another company. The likelihood of a liability arising under the guarantee is assessed as possible.

What is the correct action to be taken in the financial statements for these items?

	Create a provision	*Disclose by note only*	*No action*
A	1	2	
B		1	2
C	1 and 2		
D		1 and 2	

(2 marks)

200 **Geranium is engaged in the following research and development projects:**

Project 1   It is applying a new technology to the production of heat resistant fabric. The project is intended to last for a further 18 months after which the fabric will be used in the production of uniforms for the emergency services.

Project 2   It is considering whether a particular substance can be used as an appetite suppressant. If this is the case, it is expected be sold worldwide in chemists and pharmacies.

Project 3   It is developing a material for use in kitchens which is self cleaning and germ resistant. A competitor is currently developing a similar material and for this reason Geranium are unsure whether their project will be completed.

The costs associated with which of these projects can be capitalised?

A   Projects 1, 2 and 3

B   Projects 1 and 2

C   Project 1 only

D   Projects 1 and 3

(2 marks)

201 **Merlot, a limited liability company, is engaged in a number of research and development projects:**

Project A   A project to investigate the properties of a chemical compound

Project B   A project to develop a new process which will save time in the production of widgets. This project was started on 1 January 20X5 and met the capitalisation criteria on 31 August 20X5.

Project C   A development project which was completed on 30 June 20X5. Related costs in the statement of financial position at the start of the year were $290,000. Production and sales of the new product commenced on 1 September and are expected to last 36 months.

Costs for the year ended 31 December 20X5 are as follows:

	$
Project A	34,000
Project B costs to 31 August	78,870
Project B costs from 31 August	27,800
Project C costs to 30 June	19,800

What amount is expensed to the statement of profit or loss and other comprehensive income in respect of these projects in the year ended 31 December 20X5?

A $147,292

B $68,422

C $66,222

D $145,092 **(2 marks)**

202 **Romulus, a company, makes two changes to accounting practice at the end of 20X7:**

1 It changes the way in which it depreciates motor vehicles from 20% straight line to 25% reducing balance.

2 It starts to capitalise interest costs where allowed in accordance with the relevant standard. Previously it had adopted a policy of writing off all interest costs to the statement of profit or loss and other comprehensive income.

What is the correct way to account for these two changes?

	1	2
A	Do not adjust opening reserves	Do not adjust opening reserves
B	Do not adjust opening reserves	Adjust opening reserves
C	Adjust opening reserves	Adjust opening reserves
D	Adjust opening reserves	Do not adjust opening reserves

(2 marks)

203 **Details of two of Clooney's transactions in the year ended 31 August 20X7 are as follows:**

1 It has sold a food processing machine to a customer, Pitt. The machine has been delivered and Clooney will undertake specialist installation within the next month.

2 It has sold a number of food mixers to another customer, Damon, on credit. These have been delivered but Damon has not yet paid

For which of the transactions should revenue be recognised?

A 1 only

B 2 only

C Both 1 and 2

D Neither 1 nor 2 **(2 marks)**

204 **Where there are material non-adjusting events, a note to the financial statements should disclose:**

A   The nature of the event and the estimated financial effect

B   A letter from the solicitor

C   Nothing

D   Where the event took place   **(2 marks)**

STATEMENT OF CASH FLOWS

205 **Extracts from the accounts of Deuce showed balances as follows:**

	20X9	20X8
$1 Share capital	300,000	120,000
Share premium	260,000	100,000

A bonus issue of 1 share for every 12 held at the 20X8 year end occurred during the year and loan notes of $300,000 were issued at par. Interest of $12,000 was paid during the year.

What is the net cash inflow from financing activities?

A $480,000

B $605,000

C $617,000

D $640,000   **(2 marks)**

206 **Nobus is producing its statement of cash flows for the year ended 31 December 20X5. The accountant has identified the following balances in the financial statements:**

	$
Interest accrual b/f	4,900
Interest accrual c/f	1,200
Interest payable	20,000
Interest receivable	13,000
Preference dividend payable b/f	120,000
Preference dividends payable c/f	140,000
Dividends (statement of changes in equity)	600,000

What is the net cash flow from investing activities?

A   ($10,700)

B $13,000

C   ($603,700)

D   ($590,700)   **(2 marks)**

207 Which of the following items could appear as items in a company's statement of cash flows?

1   A bonus issue of shares.

2   A rights issue of shares.

3   The revaluation of non-current assets.

4   Dividends paid.

A   All four items

B   1, 3 and 4 only

C   2 and 4 only

D   3 only   **(2 marks)**

208 A draft statement of cash flows contains the following:

	$m
Profit before tax	22
Depreciation	8
Increase in inventories	(4)
Decrease in receivables	(3)
Increase in payables	(2)
Net cash inflow from operating activities	21

Which of the following corrections needs to be made to the calculations?

1   Depreciation should be deducted, not added.

2   Increase in inventories should be added, not deducted.

3   Decrease in receivables should be added, not deducted.

4   Increase in payables should be added, not deducted.

A   1 and 2

B   1 and 3

C   2 and 4

D   3 and 4   **(2 marks)**

209 Where, in a company's financial statements complying with International accounting standards, should you find the proceeds of non-current assets sold during the period?

A   Statement of cash flows and statement of financial position

B   Statement of changes in equity and statement of financial position

C   Statement of profit or loss and other comprehensive income and cash flow statement

D   Statement of cash flows only   **(2 marks)**

210 The figures below have been prepared for inclusion in the statement of cash flows of Bamboo.

	$
Tax and dividends paid	87,566
Increase in payables	13,899
Decrease in inventory	8,900
Redemption of loans	300,000
Increase in receivables	6,555
Reduction in cash and cash equivalents	3,211
Depreciation charge	10,600
Payments to acquire non-current assets	47,999
Proceeds from sale of non-current assets	13,100

What is the cash generated from operations?

A $331,688

B $338,110

C $425,676

D $419,254 (2 marks)

211 A business's bank balance increased by $750,000 during its last financial year. During the same period it issued shares, raising $1 million and repaid a loan of $750,000. It purchased non-current assets for $200,000 and charged depreciation of $100,000. Receivables and inventory increased by $575,000.

Its profit for the year was:

A $1,175,000

B $1,275,000

C $1,325,000

D $1,375,000 (2 marks)

212 A business had non-current assets with a carrying value of $50,000 at the start of the financial year. During the year the business sold assets that had cost $4,000 and had been depreciated by $1,500. Depreciation for the year was $9,000. The carrying value of assets at the end of the financial year was $46,000. How much cash has been invested in non-current assets during the year?

A $4,000

B $7,500

C $9,000

D $10,000 (2 marks)

213 **A business has made a profit of $8,000 but its bank balance has fallen by $5,000. This could be due to:**

A   depreciation of $3,000 and an increase in inventories of $10,000

B   depreciation of $6,000 and the repayment of a loan of $7,000

C   depreciation of $12,000 and the purchase of new non-current assets for $25,000

D   the disposal of a non-current asset for $13,000 less than its book value   **(2 marks)**

214 **A company made a profit for the year of $18,750, after accounting for depreciation of $1,250.**

During the year, non-current assets were purchased for $8,000, receivables increased by $1,000, inventories decreased by $1,800 and payables increased by $350.

The increase in cash and bank balances during the year was:

A $10,650

B $10,850

C $12,450

D $13,150   **(2 marks)**

215 **A statement of cash flows prepared in accordance with the indirect method reconciles profit before tax to cash generated from operations.**

Which of the following lists of items consists only of items that would be ADDED to profit before tax?

A   Decrease in inventory, depreciation, profit on sale of non-current assets

B   Increase in payables, decrease in receivables, profit on sale of non-current assets

C   Loss on sale of non-current assets, depreciation, increase in receivables

D   Decrease in receivables, increase in payables, loss on sale of non-current assets

                                                                                    (2 marks)

216 **In relation to statements of cash flows, which, if any, of the following are correct?**

Statement

1   The direct method of calculating net cash from operating activities leads to a different figure from that produced by the indirect method, but this is balanced elsewhere in the statement of cash flows.

2   A company making high profits must necessarily have a net cash inflow from operating activities.

3   Profits and losses on disposals of non-current assets appear as items under investing activities in the statement of cash flows.

A   Statement 1 only

B   Statement 2 only

C   Statement 3 only

D   None of the statements   **(2 marks)**

217 The movement on the plant and machinery account for X is shown below:

	$
Cost b/f	10,000
Additions	2,000
Disposals	(3,000)
Cost c/f	9,000
Depreciation b/f	2,000
Charge for the year	1,000
Disposals	(1,500)
Depreciation c/f	1,500
Carrying value b/f	8,000
Carrying value c/f	7,500

The profit on the sale of the machine was $500. What figures would appear in the statement of cash flows of X under the heading of 'Investing activities'?

A   Movement on plant account $500 and profit on disposal of $500

B   Movement on plant account $500 and proceeds on sale of plant $2,000

C   Purchase of plant $2,000 and profit on disposal of $500

D   Purchase of plant $2,000 and proceeds on sale of plant $2,000   **(2 marks)**

218 Which of the following is not an advantage of the statement of cash flows?

 A   It highlights the effect of non-cash transactions

B   It helps an assessment of the liquidity off a business

C   The numbers within it cannot be manipulated through the adoption of beneficial accounting policies

D   It helps users to estimate future cash flows   **(2 marks)**

219 Grainger is calculating its cash flow using the direct method, and has found the following information:

Cash sales	$212,500
Cash purchases	$4,600
Cash expenses	$11,200
Payables at start of year	$12,300
Payables at end of year	$14,300
Credit purchases	$123,780
Wages and salaries due at start of year	$1,500
Wages and salaries due at end of year	$2,300
Wages and salaries expense	$34,600
Inventory at start of year	$23,000
Inventory at end of year	$17,800

All sales are made for cash. What is the cash generated from operations by Grainger?

A $35,520

B $46,320

C $74,920

D $41,120   (2 marks)

220   **Howard, a limited liability company, provides the following extracts from the statement of financial position for the years ended 31 December:**

	20X6 $000	20X7 $000
Accumulated profits	72,000	82,000
10% Loan notes	30,000	40,000
Tax payable	12,000	15,000
Dividends payable	1,200	1,600

All dividends were declared and proposed **before** the year end. There was no adjustment for under/over provision for tax in the year ended 31 December 20X7. No interim dividends were paid during the year. The additional 10% loan notes were issued on 1 January 20X7.

What is the operating profit (profit before interest and tax) for the year ended 31 December 20X7?

A $29,600

B $27,200

C $30,600

D $102,600   (2 marks)

REGULATORY FRAMEWORK

221   **The IFRS Advisory Council is responsible for:**

1   giving advice to the IASB or to the trustees.

2   advising the IASB on agenda decisions.

A   1 and 2

B   1 only

C   2 only

D   Neither 1 nor two   (2 marks)

222   **Which of the following is not an enhancing qualitative characteristic of useful financial information based upon the IASB's Conceptual Framework?**

A   Comparability

B   Timeliness

C   Faithful representation

D   Understandability   (2 marks)

223 **Which of the following are true?**

1   International accounting standards are effective only if adopted by national regulatory bodies.

2   Accounting standards provide guidance on accounting for all types of transaction.

A   1 only

B   2 only

C   1 and 2

D   Neither   **(2 marks)**

224 **Which one of the following statements is correct?**

A   The going concern concept guarantees that a business will continue in operational existence for at least twelve months after the reporting date.

B   To comply with the law, the legal form of a transaction must always be reflected in financial statements

C   If a non-current asset initially recognised at cost is revalued, the surplus must be credited in the statement of cash flows

D   In times of rising prices, the use of historical cost accounting tends to understate assets and overstate profits   **(2 marks)**

225 **Which of the following is a fundamental qualitative characteristic of useful financial information per the IASB Framework?**

A   Relevance

B   Comparability

C   Timeliness

D   Verifiability   **(2 marks)**

226 **An item of inventory which had cost $5 was sold for $7. It cost the company $6 to replace the item. At the time of the sale the $6 was the item's:**

A   historical cost

B   net realisable value

C   economic value

D   current cost   **(2 marks)**

227 **The accounting concept which dictates that non-current assets should be valued at cost less accumulated depreciation, rather than at their enforced saleable value, is:**

A   Understandability

B   Relevance

C   Comparability

D   Going concern   **(2 marks)**

228 To encourage executive directors to operate in the best interests of the company, they could:

    A   be given a high basic salary

    B   receive bonuses based on both individual and company's performance

    C   be entitled to large payment on resignation

    D   be asked to attend AGMs   **(2 marks)**

229 Which of the following pairs of accounting concepts are most likely to be in conflict with one another?

    A   Comparability and understandability

    B   Accruals basis and going concern

    C   Comparability and reliability

    D   Timeliness and faithful representation   **(2 marks)**

230 The most obvious means of achieving public oversight of corporate governance is via:

    A   the company establishing a comprehensive web site

    B   publication of the Annual Report and Accounts

    C   press announcements of all significant developments

    D   shareholder access to the Annual General Meeting   **(2 marks)**

231 Which of the following statements is most accurate about the historical cost concept?

    A   It records transactions from past years

    B   It fails to take account of changing price levels over time

    C   it values assets at their cost to the business, irrespective of any depreciation or other loss in value

    D   It is no longer used in modern accounting systems   **(2 marks)**

232 In times of falling prices, the historical cost convention:

    A   understates asset values and profits

    B   understates asset values and overstates profits

    C   overstates asset values and profits

    D   overstates asset values and understates profits   **(2 marks)**

233 Who issues International Financial Reporting Standards?

    A   The IFRS Advisory Council

    B   The International Financial Reporting Interpretations Committee

    C   The International Accounting Standards Board

    D   The equity shareholders   **(2 marks)**

234 **Which of the following statements about the Framework are true?**

1   The Framework is an accounting standard.

2   It assists in harmonising accounting practice.

3   It assists national standard setters in developing national standards.

4   It assists users of the accounts to interpret financial statements.

A   1 and 2

B   2, 3 and 4

C   All 4

D   1 and 3   **(2 marks)**

235 **Which of the following are advantages of historical cost accounting?**

1   It maintains financial and physical capital.

2   The statement of financial position shows the value of the business.

3   Reported amounts are objectively verifiable.

4   The profit concept is well understood.

A   3 and 4

B   1 and 2

C   1 and 3

D   2 and 4   **(2 marks)**

GROUP FINANCIAL STATEMENTS

236 At 1 January 20X4 Yogi acquired 80% of the share capital of Bear for $1,400,000. At that date the share capital of Bear consisted of 600,000 ordinary shares of 50c each and its reserves were $50,000.

The fair value of the non-controlling interest was valued at $525,000 at the date of acquisition. In the consolidated statement of financial position of Yogi and its subsidiary Bear at 31 December 20X8, what amount should appear for goodwill?

 A $1,575,000

B $630,000

C $1,050,000

D $450,000   **(2 marks)**

237 At 1 January 20X8 Tom acquired 80% of the share capital of Jerry for $100,000. At that date the share capital of Jerry consisted of 50,000 ordinary shares of $1 each and its reserves were $30,000.

At 31 December 20X9 the reserves of Tom and Jerry were as follows:

Tom $400,000

Jerry $50,000

In the consolidated statement of financial position of Tom and its subsidiary Jerry at 31 December 20X9, what amount should appear for group reserves?

A $400,000

B $438,000

C $416,000

D $404,000 **(2 marks)**

238 At 1 January 20X6 Fred acquired 75% of the share capital of Barney for $750,000. At that date the share capital of Barney consisted of 20,000 ordinary shares of $1 each and its reserves were $10,000.

The fair value of the non-controlling interest was valued at $150,000 at 1 January 20X6. In the consolidated statement of financial position of Fred and its subsidiary Barney at 31 December 20X9, what amount should appear for goodwill?

A $150,000

B $720,000

C $870,000

D $750,000 **(2 marks)**

239 At 1 January 20X6 Gary acquired 60% of the share capital of Barlow for $35,000. At that date the share capital of Barlow consisted of 20,000 ordinary shares of $1 each and its reserves were $10,000.

At 31 December 20X9 the reserves of Gary and Barlow were as follows:

Gary $40,000

Barlow $15,000

At the date of acquisition the fair value of the non-controlling interest was valued at $25,000. In the consolidated statement of financial position of Gary and its subsidiary Barlow at 31 December 20X9, what amount should appear for non-controlling interest?

A $25,000

B $27,000

C $28,000

D $31,000 **(2 marks)**

240 At 1 January 20X8 Williams acquired 65% of the share capital of Barlow for $300,000. At that date the share capital of Barlow consisted of 400,000 ordinary shares of 50c each and its reserves were $60,000.

At 31 December 20X9 the reserves of Williams and Barlow were as follows:

Williams $200,000

Barlow $75,000

The fair value of the non-controlling interest was valued at $50,000 at the date of acquisition. In the consolidated statement of financial position of Williams and its subsidiary Barlow at 31 December 20X9, what amount should appear for non-controlling interest?

A $55,250

B $50,000

C $76,250

D $5,250   (2 marks)

241 The following extracts are provided from the statements of financial position of Dora and Diego at the year-end:

	Dora	Diego
	$000	£000
Current assets		
Inventory	200	100
Receivables	540	160
Cash	240	80
Current liabilities		
Payables	320	180

Dora's statement of financial position includes a receivable of $40,000 being due from Diego.

In the consolidated statement of financial position what will be the correct amounts for receivables and payables?

	Payables	Receivables
A	$460,000	$660,000
B	$306,000	$660,000
C	$294,000	$694,000
D	$294,000	$654,000

(2 marks)

242 Salt owns 70% of Pepper and sells goods to Pepper valued at $1,044 at a mark-up of 20%. 40% of these goods were sold on by Pepper to external parties at the year end.

What is the PURP adjustment in the group accounts?

A $69.60

B $104.40

C $125.28

D $83.52   (2 marks)

243 Stress acquired 100% of the ordinary share capital of Full on 1 October 20X7 when Full's retained earnings stood at $300,000. Full's statement of financial position at 30 September 20X9 is as follows:

	$000
Non-current assets	
Property, plant and equipment	1,800
Current assets	1,000
	2,800
Equity and reserves	
Share capital	1,600
Retained earnings	500
Current liabilities	700
	2,800

On 1 October 20X7 the fair value of land included within Full's non-current assets was $400,000 greater than the book value. Stress had non-current assets at 30 September 20X9 at book value of $2.2m.

What is the total amount for non-current assets that will appear on the consolidated statement of financial position at 30 September 20X9?

A $4,320,000

B $4,400,000

C $4,380,000

D $4,000,000

(2 marks)

Data for Questions 244 to 246

Hard acquired 80% of the ordinary share capital of Work on 1 April 20X8. The summarised statement of profit or loss for the year-ended 31 March 20X9 is as follows:

	Hard	Work
	$000	$000
Revenue	120,000	48,000
Cost of sales	84,000	40,000
Gross profit	36,000	8,000
Distribution costs	5,000	100
Administration expenses	7,000	300
Profit from operations	24,000	7,600
Investment income	150	–
Finance costs	–	400
Profit before tax	24,150	7200
Tax	6,000	1,200
Profit for the year	18,150	6,000

During the year Hard sold Work some goods for $24m, these had originally cost $18m. At the year-end Work had sold half of these goods to third parties.

244   What is the PURP adjustment for the year-ended 31 March 20X9?

    A $1,000,000

    B $6,000,000

    (C) $3,000,000

    D $7,000,000   **(2 marks)**

245   What is the total amount for revenue and cost of sales to be shown in the consolidated statement of profit or loss for the year-ended 31 March 20X9?

	Sales	Cost of sales
A	$144,000,000	$100,000,000
B	$168,000,000	$ 97,400,000
C	$192,000,000	$100,600,000
(D)	$144,000,000	$103,000,000 **(2 marks)**

246   What is the total share of profit attributable to non-controlling interest?

    (A) $1,200,000

    B $4,800,000

    C $3,630,000

    D $1,440,000   **(2 marks)**

Data for Questions 247 to 248

Really acquired 75% of the ordinary share capital of Hard on 1 January 20X9 when Hard had retained losses of $112,000. Also on that date, Really acquired 30% of the ordinary share capital of Work when Work had retained earnings of $280,000.

The summarised statement of financial position for the year-ended 31 December 20X9 is as follows:

	Really $000	Hard $000	Work $000
Non-current assets			
Property, plant and equipment	1,918	1,960	1,680
Investment in Hard	1,610		
Investment in Work	448		
	3,976	1,960	1,680
Current assets			
Inventory	760	1,280	380
Receivables	380	620	200
Cash	70	116	92
	5,186	3,976	2352
Equity and reserves			
$1 ordinary shares	2,240	1,680	1,120
Retained earnings	2,464	1,204	896
	4,704	2,884	2,016

Current liabilities

Payables	300	960	272
Taxation	182	132	64
	_____	_____	_____
	5,186	3976	2,352
	_____	_____	_____

247 What is the total amount to be shown in the consolidated statement of financial position for property, plant and equipment?

A $3,878,000

B $5,558,000

C $5,552,400

D $3,872,400   **(2 marks)**

248 What is the total reserves amount to be shown in the consolidated statement of financial position?

A $3,959,200

B $3,635,800

C $3,735,200

D $3,740,800   **(2 marks)**

249 Which of the following statements is most likely to indicate an investment by one company in another which should be recognised and accounted for as an associate?

A   Ownership of 100% of the ordinary shares of another company

B   Ownership of over 50% and less than 100% of the ordinary shares of another company

C   Ownership of between 20% and 50% of the ordinary shares of another company

D   Ownership of less than 20% of the ordinary shares in another company   **(2 marks)**

250 IFRS 10 *Consolidated financial statements* specify three necessary elements to determine whether or not one company controls another. Which of the following items is not is not one of the three necessary elements?

A   Power over the other company

B   Exposure or rights to variable returns from involvement in the other company

C   The ability to use power over the other company to affect the amount of investor returns

D   The ability to exercise significant influence over another company.   **(2 marks)**

INTERPRETATION OF FINANCIAL STATEMENTS

251 Sales are $20,000 and cost of sales are $15,400

What is the gross profit margin?

A   77%

B   129%

C   43%

D   23%   **(2 marks)**

252 The following extract relates to company X for 20X5 and 20X6:

	20X5	20X6
Revenue	20,000	26,000
Cost of sales	(15,400)	(21,050)
Gross profit	4,600	4,950
Less expenses	(2,460)	(2,770)
Operating profit	2,140	2,180

What is the operating profit margin for 20X5 and 20X6?

	20X5	20X6
A	10.7%	8.38%
B	8.38%	10.7%
C	23%	19%
D	12%	10%

                                                                                 (2 marks)

253 The following extract relates to company Y for 20X5 and 20X6:

	20X5	20X6
Statement of profit or loss extract		
Revenue	20,000	26,000
Statement of financial position extract		
Receivables	4,400	6,740
Cash	120	960

What is the receivables collection period for 20X5 and 20X6?

	20X5	20X6
A	80 days	95 days
B	82 days	108 days
C	75 days	111 days
D	95 days	80 days

                                                                                 (2 marks)

254 The following extract relates to company Z for 20X6:

	20X6
Statement of profit or loss extract	
Gross profit	15,175
Expenses	(2,460)
	————
Profit before interest and tax	12,715
Finance cost	(50)
	————
Profit before tax	12,665
Tax	(1,515)
Profit after tax	11,150

Calculate the interest cover for the year?

A   254 times

B   253 times

C   223 times

D   304 times   **(2 marks)**

255 Given selling price of $700 and gross profit mark-up of 40%, the cost price would be

A $280

B $420

C $500

D $980   **(2 marks)**

256 Sales are $220,000. Purchases are $160,000. Opening inventories is $24,000. Closing inventory is $20,000. The rate of inventory turnover (based on the average level of inventory for the period) is:

A   8.20 times

B   16.4 times

C   6.83 times

D   7.45 times   **(2 marks)**

257 The formula for calculating the rate of inventory turnover is

A   average inventories at cost divided by cost of goods sold

B   sales divided by average inventories at cost

C   sales divided by average inventories at selling price

D   cost of goods sold divided by average inventories at cost   **(2 marks)**

258 **A company has the following details extracted from its statement of financial position:**

	$000
Inventory	3,800
Receivables	2,000
Bank overdraft	200
Payables	2,000

The current ratio is:

A   Current assets: Equity

B   Total assets: current liabilities

C   Current assets: current liabilities

D   Current assets – inventory: current liabilities   **(2 marks)**

259 **A company's gearing ratio would rise if**

A   a decrease in long-term loans is less than a decrease in shareholder's funds

B   a decrease in long-term loans is more than a decrease in shareholder's funds

C   interest rates rose

D   interest rates fell   **(2 marks)**

260 **A company has the following details extracted from its statement of financial position:**

	$000
Inventory	3,800
Receivables	2,000
Bank overdraft	200
Payables	2,000

The quick (acid test) ratio is:

A   Current assets: current liabilities

B   Current assets – inventory: current liabilities

C   Current assets: bank overdraft

D   Receivables: payables   **(2 marks)**

Section 2

MULTI-TASK QUESTIONS

PAG 157

1 ICE

Ice is a limited liability company. An initial trial balance for the year ended 31 December 20X1 is presented below.

	Dr $	Cr $
Revenue		600,000
Purchases	240,000	
Administrative expenses	185,000	
Distribution expenses	75,000	
Plant and machinery – cost	120,000	
Plant and machinery – accumulated depreciation at 1 January 20X1		15,000
Trade receivables	20,500	
Allowance for receivables – 1 January 20X1		2,000
Inventory - 1 January 20X1	24,000	
Share capital		5,000
Trade payables		29,000
Retained earnings – 1 January 20X1		43,500
6% Loan – repayable 31 December 20X4		100,000
Cash	130,000	

The following notes are relevant to the preparation of the financial statements for the year ended 31 December 20X1:

The current year tax bill has been estimated at $6,000.

(i)   It has been determined that trade receivables of $1,000 are irrecoverable. No adjustment is required to the allowance for receivables.

(ii)   Depreciation on plant and machinery is charged at 20% per annum on a reducing balance basis. Depreciation is charged to cost of sales.

(iii)   The loan was taken out on 1 April 20X1. No interest has been accrued.

(iv)   Closing inventory has been correctly valued at $30,000.

(v)   A customer bought a good on credit from Ice for $500 on 10 December 20X1. They returned this good on 30 December 20X1. No entries have been posted for this return.

(vi)   Ice is being sued by an ex-employee for unfair dismissal. Legal advisers think it is probable that Ice will lose the case and that they will have to pay damages of $50,000 in 20X2. Legal costs are charged to administrative expenses.

Required:

Prepare the statement of profit or loss for Ice for the year ended 31 December 20X1 and a statement of financial position as at 31 December 20X1.   **(Total: 15 marks)**

2 WILLOW

You have been asked to help prepare the financial statements of Willow for the year ended 30 June 20X1. The company's trial balance as at 30 June 20X1 is shown below.

	Debit $000	Credit $000
Share capital		50,000
Share premium		25,000
Revaluation reserve at 1 July 20X0		10,000
Land & buildings – value/cost	120,000	
accumulated depreciation at 1 July 20X0		22,500
Plant and equipment – cost	32,000	
accumulated depreciation at 1 July 20X0		18,000
Trade and other receivables	20,280	
Trade and other payables		8,725
5% bank loan repayable 20X5		20,000
Cash and cash equivalents	2,213	
Retained earnings at 1 July 20X0		12,920
Sales		100,926
Purchases	67,231	
Distribution costs	8,326	
Administrative expenses	7,741	
Inventories at 1 July 20X0	7,280	
Dividends paid	3,000	

The following information is relevant to the preparation of the financial statements:

(i)   The inventories at the close of business on 30 June 20X1 cost $9,420,000.

(ii)   Depreciation is to be provided for the year to 30 June 20X1 as follows:

Buildings   4% per annum   Straight line basis

This should all be charged to administrative expenses

Plant and equipment   20% per annum   Reducing balance basis

This is to be apportioned as follows:

	%
Cost of sales	70
Distribution costs	20
Administrative expenses	10

Land, which is non-depreciable, is included in the trial balance at a value of $40,000,000. At 30 June 20X1, a surveyor valued it at $54,000,000. This revaluation is to be included in the financial statements for the year ended 30 June 20X1.

(iii)   It has been decided to write off a debt of $540,000 which will be charged to administrative expenses.

(iv)   Included within distribution costs is $2,120,000 relating to an advertising campaign that will run from 1 January 20X1 to 31 December 20X1.

(v)   The loan interest has not yet been accounted for.

(vi)   The tax charge for the year has been calculated as $2,700,000.

Required:

Prepare the statement of profit or loss and other comprehensive income of Willow for the year ended 30 June 20X1 and the statement of financial position as at 30 June 20X1.

(Total: 15 marks)

3   CLERC

You have been asked to help prepare the financial statements of Clerc for the year ended 31 December 20X9. The company's trial balance as at 31 December 20X9 is shown below.

	Debit	Credit
	$	$
Share capital		100,000
Share premium		20,000
Revaluation reserve at 1 January 20X9		50,000
Trade and other payables		13,882
Land & buildings – value/cost	210,000	
accumulated depreciation at 1 January 20X9		30,000
Plant and equipment – cost	88,000	
accumulated depreciation at 1 January 20X9		16,010
Trade and other receivables	8,752	
Accruals		3,029
5% bank loan repayable 20Y3		40,000
Cash and cash equivalents	6,993	
Retained earnings at 1 January 20X9		23,893
Sales		178,833
Purchases	130,562	
Distribution costs	7,009	
Administrative expenses	7,100	
Inventories at 1 January 20X9	17,331	
Bank interest received		100

The following information is relevant

(i)   The interest for the year on the bank loan has not yet been paid or accrued.

(ii)   Land, which is non-depreciable, is included in the trial balance at a value of $110,000. At 31 December 20X9 it was revalued to $150,000 and this revaluation is to be included in the financial statements.

(iii)   Depreciation is to be provided for the year to 31 December 20X9 as follows:

Buildings	10% per annum	Straight line basis
Plant and equipment	20% per annum	Reducing balance basis

As part of the building contains the office accommodation, the depreciation for the 'Buildings' is apportioned as follows:

	%
Cost of sales	40
Administrative expenses	60

(iv)   Included in trade receivables is a balance of $1,720 that is considered to be irrecoverable due to the customer going into administration and the Directors of Clerc feel this should be written off.

(v)   The inventories at the close of business on 31 December 20X9 were valued at cost of $19,871. Included in this balance was an inventory line costing $4,000 that, due to change in legislation, is now illegal. Clerc could rectify the items at a cost of $2,500 and plans to do so. The items usually retail to customers at $6,000.

(vi)   The tax charge for the year has been calculated as $7,162.

Required:

Prepare the statement of profit or loss and other comprehensive income of Clerc for the year ended 31 December 20X9 and the statement of financial position as at 31 December 20X9.

(15 marks)

4   CARBON

Carbon is a limited liability company. An initial trial balance for the year ended 31 December 20X5 is presented below.

	Dr	Cr
	$	$
Revenue		450,000
Purchases	180,000	
Administrative expenses	140,000	
Distribution expenses	56,000	
Plant and machinery – cost	150,000	
Plant and machinery – accumulated depreciation at 1 January 20X5		30,000
Trade receivables	36,000	
Allowance for receivables – 1 January 20X5		2,500
Inventory - 1 January 20X5	33,000	
Share capital		10,000
Trade payables		32,000
Retained earnings – 1 January 20X5		25,500
8% Loan – repayable 31 December 20X9		50,000
Cash	5,000	
	–––––––	–––––––
	600,000	600,000
	–––––––	–––––––

The following notes are relevant to the preparation of the financial statements for the year ended 31 December 20X5:

(i)   The current year tax charge has been estimated at $5,000.

(ii)   It has been determined that trade receivables of $1,500 are irrecoverable. In addition, it was decided that the allowance for receivables should be increased by $1,000.

(iii)   Depreciation on plant and machinery is charged at 20% per annum on a reducing balance basis. Depreciation is charged to cost of sales.

(iv)   The loan was taken out on 1 October 20X5. No interest has been accrued.

(v)   Closing inventory has been correctly valued at $27,000.

(vi)   A customer bought goods on credit from Carbon for $1,000 on 5 December 20X5. The customer returned these goods on 28 December 20X5. No entries have been posted for this return.

(vii) Carbon is being sued by a customer regarding the sale of goods that the customer believes to be defective. Legal advisers think that it is probable that Carbon will lose the case and that they will have to pay damages of $20,000 in 20X6. Legal expenses are charged to administrative expenses.

Prepare a statement of profit or loss of Carbon the year ended 31 December 20X5 and a statement of financial position as at 31 December 20X5. **(Total: 15 marks)**

5 PATTY AND SELMA

The statements of profit or loss for two companies, Patty and Selma, for the year ended 31 December 20X1 are presented below:

	Patty	Selma
	$000	$000
Revenue	987	567
Cost of sales	(564)	(335)
Gross profit	423	232
Administrative expenses	(223)	(122)
Operating profit	200	110
Finance costs	(50)	(30)
Profit before tax	150	80
Taxation	(40)	(25)
Profit for the year	110	55

The following notes are relevant to the preparation of the consolidated financial statements: Patty bought 70% of the ordinary shares in Selma several years ago.

(i) During the year ended 31 December 20X1, Selma sold goods to Patty for $120,000 making a cost mark up of 20%. One quarter of these goods remained in the inventory of Patty at the year end.

Required

Using the individual company financial statements, calculate the following ratios for Patty and Selma for the year ended 31 December 20X1:

(i) **Gross profit margin**

(ii) **Operating profit margin**

(iii) **Interest cover** **(6 marks)**

Prepare a consolidated statement of profit or loss for the year ended 31 December 20X1.

(9 marks)

(Total: 15 marks)

6   CUBE AND PRISM

The statements of financial position for Cube and Prism as at 31 December 20X1 are presented below:

	Cube $	Prism $
Assets		
Non-current assets		
Property, plant and equipment	270,000	179,000
Investments	300,000	–
Current assets		
Inventories	95,000	50,000
Trade and other receivables	110,000	99,000
Cash and cash equivalents	8,000	51,000
Total Assets	783,000	379,000
Equity and liabilities		
Equity		
Share capital	100,000	50,000
Retained earnings	435,000	209,000
Non-current liabilities		
Loans	200,000	70,000
Current liabilities		
Trade and other payables	48,000	50,000
Total equity and liabilities	783,000	379,000

The following notes are relevant to the preparation of the consolidated financial statements:

(i)   Cube acquired 75% of the ordinary shares of Prism for $300,000 several years ago. At the acquisition date, the retained earnings of Prism were $120,000. The fair value of the non-controlling interest at the date of acquisition was $55,000.

(ii)   The fair values of the net assets of Prism at the acquisition date approximated their carrying values, with the exception of some land. This land was held in the accounts of Prism at its cost of $100,000 but was estimated to have a fair value of $170,000. This land is still held at 31 December 20X1.

(iii)   During the year, Cube sold goods to Prism for $30,000 making a gross profit margin on the sale of 30%. One third of these goods are still included in the inventories of Prism.

Required

(a)   **Using the individual financial statements, calculate the following ratios for Cube and Prism for the year ended 31 December 20X1:**

(i)   **The quick ratio (x:1)**

(ii)   **Gearing (in terms of the percentage of capital employed represented by borrowings)**

All ratios should be calculated to one decimal place.   **(4 marks)**

(b)   **Prepare the consolidated statement of financial position for the Cube group as at 31 December 20X1.**   **(11 marks)**

(Total: 15 marks)

7   BRYSON AND STOPPARD

Bryson acquired 75% of the issued share capital of Stoppard on 1 April 20X0 for $8,720,000. At that date Stoppard had issued share capital of $4,800,000 and retained earnings of $670,000.

Extracts of the statements of financial position for the two companies one year later at 31 March 20X1 are as follows:

	Bryson $000	Stoppard $000
ASSETS		
Investment in Stoppard	8,720	
Non-current assets	11,280	3,670
Current assets	5,760	5,010
Total assets	25,760	8,680
EQUITY AND LIABILITIES	$000	$000
Equity		
Share capital	9,200	4,800
Retained earnings	12,480	1,290
Total equity	21,680	6,090
Non-current liabilities	1,440	1,180
Current liabilities	2,640	1,410
Total liabilities	4,080	2,590
Total equity and liabilities	25,760	8,680

The following information is relevant to the preparation of the consolidated financial statements:

(i)   At acquisition, the fair value of land owned by Stoppard exceeded its cost by $1,000,000. This land is still owned at 31 March 20X1.

(ii)   During the year Bryson sold goods to Stoppard for $960,000 making a profit of $400,000. Three quarters of the goods remained in Stoppard's inventory at the year end. Stoppard still owes half the amount payable to Bryson

(iii)   At 1 April 20X0, the fair value of the non-controlling interest at the date of acquisition was $2,200,000.

Required

(c)   Calculate the current ratio for Bryson and Stoppard as at 31 March 20X1.   **(2 marks)**

(d)   **Prepare the consolidated statement of financial position for Bryson plc and its subsidiary undertaking as at 31 March 20X1.**   **(13 marks)**

(Total 15 marks)

8   PEN AND STAPLE

The statements of profit or loss for two companies, Pen and Staple, for the year ended 31 December 20X4 are presented below:

	Pen	Staple
	$000	$000
Revenue	1,500	700
Cost of sales	(775)	(370)
Gross profit	725	330
Administrative expenses	(317)	(135)
Operating profit	408	195
Finance costs	(60)	(35)
Profit before tax	348	160
Taxation	(96)	(45)
Profit for the year	252	115

The following notes are relevant to the preparation of the consolidated financial statements:

(i)   Pen bought 70% of the ordinary shares in Staple on 1 January 20X1.

(ii)   During the year ended 31 December 20X4, Staple sold goods to Pen for $150,000 making a mark up on cost of 20%. One fifth of these goods remained in the inventory of Pen at the year end.

Required

(a)   **Using the individual company financial statements, calculate the following ratios for Pen and Staple for the year ended 31 December 20X4:**

(i)   **Gross profit margin**

(ii)   **Operating profit margin**

(iii)   **Interest cover**   **(6 marks)**

(b)   **Prepare a consolidated statement of profit or loss for the Pen group for the year ended 31 December 20X4.**   **(9 marks)**

(Total: 15 marks)

9   PEBBLE AND STONE

The statements of financial position for Pebble and Stone as at 31 December 20X6 are presented below:

	Pebble $	Stone $
Assets		
Non-current assets		
Property, plant and equipment	300,000	225,000
Investments	400,000	–
Current assets		
Inventories	80,000	75,000
Trade and other receivables	60,000	140,000
Cash and cash equivalents	10,000	25,000
Total Assets	850,000	465,000
Equity and liabilities		
Equity		
Share capital	80,000	60,000
Share premium	20,000	10,000
Retained earnings	295,000	250,000
Non-current liabilities		
Loans	300,000	85,000
Current liabilities		
Trade and other payables	155,000	60,000
Total equity and liabilities	850,000	465,000

The following notes are relevant to the preparation of the consolidated financial statements:

(i)   Pebble acquired 80% of the ordinary shares of Stone for $300,000 on 1 January 20X2. At the acquisition date, the retained earnings of Stone were $150,000. The fair value of the non-controlling interest in Stone at the date of acquisition was $80,000.

(i)   At the date of acquisition, the fair values of the net assets of Stone approximated their carrying values, with the exception of some land. This land was held in the accounts of Stone at its cost of $150,000 but was estimated to have a fair value of $180,000. This land is still owned by Stone at 31 December 20X6.

(ii)   During the year, Pebble sold goods to Stone for $50,000 making a gross profit margin on the sale of 25%. Two fifths of these goods are still included in the inventories of Stone at 31 December 20X6.

Required

(a) Prepare the consolidated statement of financial position for the Pebble group as at 31 December 20X6.   **(11 marks)**

(b) Pebble is considering making an investment in another company, Archive, which would be accounted for as an associate. Which of the following factors would be relevant when accounting for an associate?

Control of Archive

Significant influence in Archive

Owning the majority of the ordinary shares of Archive

Owning between 20% and 50% of the ordinary shares of Archive

Accounting for goodwill

Accounting of non-controlling interests   **(4 marks)**

                                                                          (Total: 15 marks)

Section 3

ANSWERS TO MULTIPLE CHOICE TEST QUESTIONS

INTRODUCTION TO FINANCIAL REPORTING

1   D

- The directors of a company run the company, however are not liable for its losses.

- A sole trader business is owned and operated by the proprietor (sole trader)

- Partners are jointly and severally liable for any losses of the business.

- A company is owned by the shareholders (members) and run by the directors/ management team.

2   B

Management accounts are:

- Sufficiently detailed for management to control the business and plan for the future.

- Normally prepared monthly (on a rolling basis).

- Not mandatory.

- Based on past performance as well as budgets and forecasts.

- Relevant to managers.

3   C

- An employee is interested in whether a business will continue into the future in order to assess their job security. This is a prime concern of an employee.

- Employees may be able to invest in shares in the company they work for, in which case profitability will be of interest to them. This is, however, not always the case.

- Employees may also be interested in the effect of the business on the local environment and community, and the performance of competitors however these are generally secondary concerns.

4   A

Management require very detailed information in order to make informed decisions with regard to operations (e.g. whether to shut down a particular product line or source new suppliers).

Other parties need far less detail:

- Investors are interested in profitability and the security of their investment.

- The government is interested in profits (for tax purposes) and sales performance (in order to assess how the economy is performing).

- Lenders are interested in whether a business is solvent and able to repay their debt.

5   A

- Accounting involves recording transactions as they occur and then summarising them in the form of the financial statements.

- Financial accounting describes the production of accounts for external use.

6   C

7   C

Both financial and management accounts are equally accurate.

STATEMENT OF FINANCIAL POSITION AND STATEMENT OF PROFIT OR LOSS

8   B

	$	$
Sales (β)		25,600
Cost of sales		
Opening inventory	1,500	
Purchases	12,950	
Inventory drawings	(75)	
Closing inventory	(900)	
		(13,475)
Gross profit		12,125

9   B

- The definition of an asset requires that it is controlled by an entity. Whether the item is owned outright or paid for are irrelevant as long as control is achieved.

- An amount owed by an entity is a liability.

10   A

Opening net assets + capital injections + profit − drawings = closing net assets

Opening net assets + $9,800 + $8,000 − $4,200 = $19,000

Opening net assets = Opening capital = $5,400

11   D

Capital = net assets

- If a supplier is paid by cheque, assets reduce as do liabilities, therefore there is no change to net assets.

- If raw materials or non-current assets are purchased on credit, assets increase as do liabilities; again there is no change to net assets.

- If wages are paid in cash, assets decrease (the other effect is to reduce profits which in turn reduces capital).

12   B

The loan was included as a current liability, but should be treated as a non-current liability. Correcting the error will reduce total current liabilities, and this will increase net current assets (= current assets minus current liabilities).

13   B

Profit is the increase in net assets between the beginning and end of the period, plus drawings taken out of the business, minus new equity introduced in the period (which is not profit).

14   C

The separate business entity concept means that accounting information should only relate to the business, not the owner of the business. Therefore goods taken by the owner must be treated as drawings and removed from the inventory of the business.

15   D

Current assets	$	Current liabilities	$
Receivables	23,800	Overdraft	3250
Allowances for receivables	(1,500)	Payables	31,050
Inventory	12,560	Rent accrual	1,200
Petty cash	150	Loan	25,000
	35,010		60,500

- The bank statement shows a debit balance, indicating an overdraft (from the bank's perspective, they are owed money by Andrew).

- The first instalment of the loan (25%) is due within 12 months and so shown as a current liability.

16   A

Assets	=	Liabilities	+	Capital
At start of week:				
15,700	=	11,200	+	4,500(β)
1 May				
+300		+ 300		+ 1,400
+1,400				
3 May				
−750				− 750
4 May				
−400				− 400
7 May				
+1,200				+ 1,200
−600				− 600
At end of week:				
16,850	=	11,500	+	5,350

DOUBLE ENTRY BOOKKEEPING

17   B

- The computer does not qualify as inventory drawings as it is for the use of Oscar's daughter in her role as administrator to the business.

- The computer is being transferred from inventory to non-current assets by debiting the non-current assets account. It is no longer part of cost of sales and is removed from cost of sales by a credit.

18   B

- Drawings, carriage outwards (an expense), prepayments, Carriage inwards (expense) and opening inventory are all debit balances.

- Accruals, rental income and purchase returns are all credit balances.

19   C

20   C

21   D

	$	$
Sales		256,800
Cost of sales		
Opening inventory	13,400	
Purchases	145,000	
Carriage in	2,300	
Closing inventory	(14,200)	
		(146,500)
Gross profit		110,300
Expenses		(76,000)
Discount allowed		(1,950)
Discount received		3,900
Net profit		36,250

22   B

Bank

	$		$
Balance b/f	1,780	Drawings (4 × $200)	800
Receipt after discount	570		
Receipt from customer	400		
Bankings	1,200	Balance c/f	3,150
	3,950		3,950

Settlement discounts are given if a credit customer pays within a certain time. If a $30 settlement discount is taken, then the net amount of $570 must have been received during the month.

23   D

Bank

	$		$
Returns of goods purchased for cash	50	Overdraft at start of month	1,340
Rental income	1,300	Payments to credit suppliers	990
Receipts from customers	4,400	Reimbursement of petty cash float	45
		Payment of electricity bill	700
		Balance c/f	2,675
	5,750		5,750

24   C

INVENTORY

25 **A**

- The inventory should be valued at the lower of cost and NRV.

- Cost is $500.

- NRV is $1,200 – $250 = $950.

- The correct valuation is therefore $500.

26 **A**

Opening inventory + units purchased		440
Units sold		(290)
		————
Closing inventory (units)		150
		————

FIFO	Closing inventory: 150 units @ $2.78	$417
AVCO	Weighted average cost	$
	100 units @ $2.52	252
	140 units @ $2.56	358
	200 units @ $2.78	556
	———	————
	440	1,166
	———	————

Average cost per unit	1,166 = $2.65
	————
	440
Closing inventory: 150 units @ $2.65	$397.50
FIFO higher by (417 – 397.50)	$19.50

The periodic weighted requires the total cost of the inventory to be divided by the total units in the period to determine the weighted average cost for the period. This weighted average figure will then be used to value the inventory.

The continuous weighted method requires the weighted average to be calculated every time there is a purchase.

27 **B**

- If prices have fallen during the year, AVCO will give a higher value of closing inventory than FIFO, which values goods for resale at the latest prices.

- Where the value of closing inventory is higher, profits are higher.

28 **D**

- The number of units held at the year end is 1,180 (1,200 – 20)

The sale on 31 December provides evidence of a net realisable value $2 below cost. Therefore each unit should be valued at its net realisable value:

1,180 units × $48 = $56,640

29   C

- Inventory should be valued at the lower of cost and net realisable value. Replacement cost is irrelevant.

30   C

- Where inventory is included in purchases at cost and closing inventory at cost, the effect on profit is nil (the same amount is both a debit and a credit in the statement of profit or loss).

- In this case, only the credit is recorded (closing inventory). Therefore profit is overstated by the cost of the fabric.

- Inventory is neither under nor overstated, since the inclusion of the fabric is correct.

31   A

- Inventory drawings are credited to purchases in order to remove them from cost of sales, as these goods have not been sold.

32   B

At the year end:

1   Opening inventory must be removed from the statement of financial position inventory account (a credit) and expensed to the statement of profit or loss as part of cost of sales (a debit).

2   Closing inventory must be debited on to the statement of financial position as an asset and removed from the cost of sales (a credit)

33   B

	$
Value at 7 July 20X6	38,950
Sales since year end (100/125 × $6,500)	5,200
Purchase since year end	(4,250)
	———
Value at 30 June 20X6	39,900
	———

34   B

	Items	Unit value	
		$	$
Opening inventory	6	15	90
January: purchases	10	19.80	198
	16	18	288
February: sales	(10)	18	(180)
	6	18	108
March: purchases	20	24.50	490
	26	23	598
March: sales	(5)	23	(115)
	21	23	483

	$
Sales (15 × $30)	450
Cost of sales ($180 + $115)	(295)
Gross profit	155

35   C

Date		Units	Unit value	Inventory value
			$	$
1 October	Opening inventory	60		720
8 October	Purchase 40 units at $15	40		600
14 October	Purchase 50 units at $18	50		900
		150	14.80	2,220
21 October	Sold 75 units: cost	(75)	14.80	(1,110)
31 October	Closing inventory	75	14.80	1,110

36   A

The net realisable value of inventory items is the selling price less the 4% commission payable.

	NRV	Lower of cost or NRV
	$	$
Henry VII	2,784	2,280
Dissuasion	3,840	3,840
John Bunion	1,248	1,248
		————
		7,368
		————

37   D

The closing inventory of 12 items (15 – 5 + 10 – 8) comprise

	$
10 items at $3.50 each	35.00
2 items at $3 each	6.00
	————
Cost on a FIFO basis is	41.00
	————

38   B

If the inventory was not included in the original count of closing inventory, closing inventory will be increased by $1,000 (the lower of cost and net realisable value). Since closing inventory is $1,000 higher, the cost of sales is $1,000 lower and profit $1,000 higher.

39   B

	Net realisable value	Lower of cost or NRV	Units	Value
	$	$		$
Basic	8	6	200	1,200
Super	8	8	250	2,000
Luxury	10	10	150	1,500
				————
Total value				4,700
				————

40   A

When prices are rising, FIFO will give a higher valuation for closing inventory, because the closing inventory will consist of the most recently-purchased items. Higher closing inventory means lower cost of sales and higher profit.

SALES TAX

41 A

	$
Price	600
Less: trade discount (5% × $600)	(30)
	570
Less: Cash/settlement discount (3% × $570)	(17.10)
	552.90
Sales tax at 17.5 × $552.90	= $96.76

Sales tax is always charged on the selling price net of:

- actual trade (bulk buy) discounts given

- settlement (prompt payment) discounts, regardless of whether they are taken.

42 C

Sales tax

	$		$
		Balance b/f	23,778
Tax on purchases		Tax on sales	
$\dfrac{17.5\%}{117.5\%} \times \$590,790$	87,990	17.5% × $800,000	140,000
Balance c/f	75,788		
	163,778		163,778
		Balance b/f	75,788

43 B

Sales tax

	$		$
Tax on purchases (input tax)		Tax on sales (output tax)	4,112.5
($18,000 × 17.5%)	3,150.0	($27,612.5 × 17.5/117.5)	
Balance c/f	962.5		
	4,112.5		4,112.5
		Balance b/f	962.5

44   C

	$
Sales net of sales tax	90,000
Purchases net of sales tax	(72,000)
	18,000
Tax payable @ 10%	$1,800

As sales exceed purchases, the excess sales tax is payable to the tax authorities.

45   D

Sales tax

	$		$
Tax on purchases	6,000	Balance b/f	3,400
Bank	2,600	Tax on sales	10,500
Balance c/f	5,300		
	13,900		13,900
		Balance b/f	5,300

Tax on sales (outputs) = 17.5% × $60,000 = $10,500

Tax on purchases (inputs) = (17.5/117.5) × $40,286 = $6,000

46   B

Sales are recorded exclusive of sales tax in the statement of profit or loss.

47   B

The receivables account should be debited with the full amount payable, including the tax. The entry in the sales account should be for the sales value excluding sales tax. Sales tax payable to the tax authorities should be credited to the sales tax account (liability = credit balance).

48   A

The receivables account should be credited with the full amount of the sales return, including the tax. The Sales returns account should be debited with the value of the returns excluding the sales tax. The sales tax account should be debited with the amount of tax on the returns (since the tax is no longer payable).

49   C

The supplier is owed the full amount of the invoice, including the sales tax, so the credit entry in the supplier account must be $9,200. The non-current asset account is recorded at cost excluding the sales tax. The input tax is recoverable, so debit the sales tax account with $1,200.

50   A

- If input tax (tax on purchases) exceeds output tax (tax on sales), the difference is recoverable from the tax authorities.

- Sales and purchases are reported net of sales tax.

- Sales tax cannot be recovered on certain expenses (such as client entertaining) and purchases (such as cars).

ACCRUALS AND PREPAYMENTS

51   A

Rental income (property 1 and 2)

	$		$
Balance b/f	5,400	Balance b/f	12,300
Statement of profit or loss rental income (β)	453,600	Cash received (280,000 +160,000)	440,000
Balance c/f	6,700	Balance c/f	13,400
	———		———
	465,700		465,700
	———		———
Balance b/f	13,400	Balance b/f	6,700

52   D

Rental income

	$		$
Balance b/f	42,300	Balance b/f	102,600
Statement of profit or loss (β)	858,600	Cash received	838,600
Balance c/f	88,700	Balance c/f	48,400
	———		———
	989,600		989,600
	———		———

53   A

		$
Statement of profit or loss	9/12 × $10,800	8,100
	3/12 × $12,000	3,000
		———
		11,100
		———
Statement of financial position prepayment	9/12 × $12,000	9,000

54   D

Statement of profit or loss (5/12 × $24,000) + (7/12 × $30,000) = $27,500

Statement of financial position $7,500 paid on 1 January therefore amount prepaid by tenant is:

2/3 × $7,500 = $5,000. For Vine this is prepaid/deferred income, i.e. income received in advance – a liability.

55   A

Motor expenses

	$		$
Balance b/f (insurance)	80	Balance b/f (petrol)	95
Cash paid – petrol	95		
– other bills	245	Statement of profit or loss (β)	385
Balance c/f (petrol)	120	Balance c/f (insurance)	60
	540		540

The insurance prepayment covers 4 months as at the start of September. Therefore there must be a prepayment of 3 months at the end of September.

56   A

Charge to statement of profit or loss $1,800 × 7/12 = $1,050

Prepayment $1,800 × 5/12 = $750

57   C

The accrual for May and June 20X3 is assumed to be 2/3 × $840 = $560.

Electricity expenses

	$		$
Bank	600	Opening balance b/f	300
Bank	720		
Bank	900		
Bank	840		
Closing balance c/f	560	Statement of profit or loss	3,320
	3,620		3,620

58   C

The premium for the year 1 July 20X2 to 30 June 20X3 was $13,200 × 1/1.1 = $12,000

Statement of profit or loss charge:

6 months at $12,000 plus 6 months at $13,200 = $6,000 + $6,600 = $12,600

59 B

The charge in the statement of profit or loss will be the amount of interest incurred from 1 January (when the loan was taken out) to 30 September (the year end) i.e. $9/12 \times 12\% \times \$100,000 = \$9,000$. This represents three interest payments.

However, as only two interest payments were made (1 April and 1 July) the third payment due to be made on 1 October, which relates to the three months to 30 September, will be accrued: $3/12 \times 12\% \times \$100,000 = \$3,000$.

60 C

	$
Prepayment brought forward at the start of the year	10,000
Payment during the year	36,000
	———
	46,000
Less: Prepayment carried forward at the year end (7 months, therefore $36,000 × 7/12)	(21,000)
	———
Charge for insurance in the statement of profit or loss	25,000
	———

61 B

- Accrued income is income not yet received for a service already provided (income received in arrears). The correct double entry to record accrued income is:

Dr Accrued income (statement of financial position)

Cr Income (statement of profit or loss)

It therefore increases rather than decreases profit.

IRRECOVERABLE DEBTS AND ALLOWANCES FOR RECEIVABLES

62 D

Receivables ledger control account

	$		$
Balance b/f	34,500	Cash received	229,900
Credit sales (β)	278,090	Contra	1,200
		Discounts allowed	17,890
		Irrecoverable debts	18,600
		Balance c/f	45,000
	———		———
	312,590		312,590
	———		———
Balance b/f	45,000		

Total sale = Credit sales + Cash sales

= $278,090 + $24,000

= $302,090

Note:

- Discounts received are relevant to the payables ledger control account.

- The double entry for the increase in allowance for receivables is:

Dr Irrecoverable debts expense   12,500

Cr Allowance for receivables   12,500

63   B

Receivables ledger control account

	$		$
Balance b/f	84,700	Contra with payables ledger control account	5,000
Credit sales	644,000	Irrecoverable debts	4,300
		Discounts allowed	30,780
		Cash received from credit customers	595,000
		Balance c/f	93,620
	728,700		728,700

- The double entry for a contra is Dr payables ledger control account (payables) and Cr receivables ledger control account (receivables).

- Discounts received are relevant to payables not receivables.

- Cash sales should not feature in the receivables ledger control account.

- The correct double entry for the increase in the allowance for receivables is Dr irrecoverable debts expense and Cr allowance for receivables.

64   A

	$	Allowance $	Expense $
Receivables balance (draft)	58,200		
Irrecoverable debts	(8,900)		8,900
	49,300		
Specific allowance: Carroll	(1,350)	1,350	
Juffs	(750)	750	
	47,200		
General allowance at 3% × $47,200		1,416	
Allowance c/f		3,516	
Allowance b/f		5,650	
Decrease in allowance		2,134	(2,134)
Total expense			6,766

65   B

Receivables ledger control account

	$		$
Balance b/f (W)	13,150		
Sales	125,000	Cash	115,500
		Irrecoverable debts	7,100
		Balance c/f	15,550
	138,150		138,150

	b/f $	c/f $
Gross receivables	13,150	15,550
Allowance	(1,150)	(2,100)
Net receivables	12,000	13,450

66   B

- The write off of debts will reduce the gross receivables balance by $72,000 to $766,000.

- The allowance is to be adjusted to $60,000 (hence an adjustment of $12,000).

- The net balance is therefore $766,000 less $60,000, i.e. $706,000.

67   A

Year end receivables	5% × $7,000,000	=	$350,000
Year end allowance for receivables	4% × $350,000	=	$14,000
Allowance at start of year	100/120 × $14,000	=	$11,667
Increase in allowance		**=**	**$2,333**

Irrecoverable debts expense

	$		$
Write off of irrecoverable debts	3,200	Recovery of irrecoverable debts	450
Increase in allowance	2,333	Statement of profit or loss (β)	5,083
	———		———
	5,533		5,533
	———		———

68   A

Trade receivables

	$		$
Balance b/f	10,000	Receipts	90,000
Sales	100,000	Discounts allowed	800
Irrecoverable debts recovered	1,000	Balance c/f	20,200
	———		———
	111,000		111,000
	———		———

69   A

When a debt is written off as irrecoverable, the transaction is recorded as:

Dr Irrecoverable debts account (expense)

Cr Receivable account.

Any subsequent change to the allowance for receivables should be dealt with as a separate matter.

70   A

- Cash sales do not affect receivables.

- Discounts received affect payables, not receivables.

- The allowance for receivables does not affect the amount of receivables, but specific irrecoverable debts written off do affect receivables.

Receivables

	$		$
Balance b/f	37,500	Discounts allowed	15,750
Sales (credit)	357,500	Irrecoverable debts written off	10,500
		Bank (β)	329,750
		Balance c/f	39,000
	———		———
	395,000		395,000
	———		———

71   A

- Receivables (5% of $2 million) = $100,000.

- Required allowance for receivables (4% of $100,000) = $4,000.

- Current allowance for receivables = $4,000 × ¾ = $3,000.

- Increase in allowance = $1,000.

- An increase in the allowance for receivables reduces profits.

72   A

	$
Irrecoverable debts written off (800 + 550)	1,350
Irrecoverable debt recovered	(350)
Reduction in allowance for receivables	(200)
Charge to statement of profit or loss	800

73   B

The allowance for receivables will reduce the book value of receivables. An increase in an allowance for receivables will therefore reduce net current assets.

74   A

	$	$	$
Receivables balance		230,000	
Specific allowance – Emily		(450)	450
– Lulu		(980)	980
		228,570	
General allowance @ 5% of $228,570			11,429
Total allowance at end of year			12,859
Allowance b/f			(11,700)
Increase in allowance = Dr to statement of profit or loss			1,159

75   D

The provision of credit will not improve the cash flow position of the business, rather it may result in a deterioration of cash flow. This is particularly true as some customers will be late in paying and others will not pay at all.

76   C

An aged receivables analysis is a list of how much each credit customer owes and how old their debt is. It enables the credit control function to identify which customers to chase, and also helps in the calculation of the allowance for receivables at the year end.

NON-CURRENT ASSETS

77   C

Asset register	$	Ledger accounts	$
Carrying value per question	85,600	Carrying value per question	130,000
Addition of land	30,000	Disposal at carrying value	(14,400)
	115,600		115,600

78   A

		$
1.1.X4	Cost	235,000
	Depreciation at 30%	(70,500)
y/e 31.12.X4	Carrying value	164,500
	Depreciation at 30%	(49,350)
y/e 31.12.X5	Carrying value	115,150
	Depreciation at 20%	(34,545)
y/e 31.12.X6	Carrying value	80,605
	Accumulated depreciation (70,500 + 49,350 + 34,545)	154,395

Therefore

(1)   Uplift cost account to valuation

Dr Cost $65,000

(2)   Remove depreciation to date

Dr Accumulated depreciation $154,395

(3)   Send the balance to the revaluation reserve

Cr Revaluation reserve $219,395

79   D

A non-current asset register is a detailed schedule of non-current assets, and is not another name for non-current asset ledger accounts in the general ledger.

80   C

81   B

			$
Depreciation on additions:	20% × $48,000 × 6/12	=	4,800
Depreciation on disposals:	20% × $84,000 × 9/12	=	12,600
Depreciation on other assets:	20% × (960,000 – 84,000)	=	175,200
			192,600

82   C

	$
Cost of plant	48,000
Delivery	400
Modifications	2,200
	50,600

The warranty cost cannot be capitalised. This is a revenue expense which must be debited to the statement of profit or loss.

83   B

		$
Year 1	Cost	2,400.0
	Depreciation at 20%	(480.0)
Year 2	Carrying value	1,920.0
	Depreciation at 20%	(384.0)
Year 3	Carrying value	1,536.0
	Depreciation at 20%	(307.2)
Year 4	Carrying value	1,228.8
	Sale proceeds	1,200.0
	Loss on disposal	(28.8)

84   B

	$	$
Original balance		125,000
Carrying value of assets sold:		
Proceeds	9,000	
Less: Profit	(2,000)	
		(7,000)
Adjusted balance		118,000

85   C

A non-current asset should be measured initially at its cost. 'Cost' means the amounts incurred to acquire the asset and bring it into working condition for its intended use. These include the purchase cost, initial delivery and handling costs, installation costs and professional fees. Costs of testing whether the asset is working properly may be included, but costs of staff training are not.

	$
Purchase cost of machine	80,000
Installation	5,000
Testing	1,000
	86,000

86   A

	$
Cost	5,000
Year 1 (20% × 5,000)	(1,000)
Year 2 (20% × 4,000)	(800)
Year 3 (20% × 3,200)	(640)
Carrying value at time of disposal	2,560
Sale proceeds	2,200
Loss on disposal	360

Note: The residual value does not impact reducing balance calculations of depreciation.

87 C

	$m
Non-current assets at cost	10.40
Accumulated depreciation	(0.12)
Carrying value	10.28
Revaluation amount	15.00
Transfer to revaluation reserve	4.72

88 D

Painting and replacing windows are maintenance and repairs, and so are classified as 'revenue expenditure' and must be expensed through the statement of profit or loss. The purchase of a car for resale means that the car is an item of inventory for the business, not a non-current asset. Legal fees incurred in purchasing a building are included in the cost of the building, and so are part of the non-current asset cost, i.e. capital expenditure.

89 D

Disposals account

	$		$
Cost	12,000	Accumulated depreciation	7,200
		(3 yrs × 20% × $12,000)	
Profit (β)	200	Proceeds (part exchange allowance)	5,000
	12,200		12,200

90 C

	Cost	Accum dep'n	Carrying value
	$000	$000	$000
Opening balance	860	397	
Disposal	(80)	(43)	
	780	354	
Purchase	180		
	960		
Depreciation (10%)		96	
		450	
CV = 960 – 450			510

91   C

92   C

1 Jan – 30 June: 3% of $380,000 × 6/12 = $5,700

1 July – 31 December: 3% of $450,000 × 6/12 = $6,750

Charge for the year: $5,700 + $6,750 = $12,450

93   D

Do not include the road tax in the cost of the car. Road tax is a revenue expense item.

	$
Cost of asset	10,000
Depreciation 20X1 (25%)	(2,500)
	7,500
Depreciation 20X2 (25%)	(1,875)
	5,625
Depreciation 20X3 (25%)	(1,406)
	4,219
Depreciation 20X4 (25%)	(1,055)
Carrying value at time of disposal	3,164
Disposal value	5,000
Profit on disposal	1,836

94   D

The reducing balance method charges more depreciation in earlier years than in later years. It is therefore appropriate to use for assets such as motor vehicles that lose a large part of their value in the earlier years of their life.

95   C

Annual depreciation = $(40,000 – 10,000)/6 years = $5,000.

The machine was held for four years before disposal, giving accumulated depreciation of 4 × $5,000 = $20,000.

When the machine was sold, its carrying value was $40,000 – $20,000 = $20,000. It was sold for $15,000, giving a loss on disposal of $5,000.

	$
Accumulated depreciation	20,000
Loss on disposal	5,000
Total charged over the life of the machine	25,000

96   B

Initial depreciation charge p.a. $\dfrac{\$20,000-\$500}{10\,\text{years}}$ = $1,950

Carrying value at date of change $20,000 – $1,950 = $18,050

New depreciation charge (for y/e 30 June X9 onwards) $\dfrac{\$18,050}{5\,\text{yrs}}$ = $3,610

Note that the revision of estimations takes place in the year ended 30 June 20X9 before the depreciation for that year is charged.

FROM TRIAL BALANCE TO FINANCIAL STATEMENTS

97   C

	$	$
Plant and machinery	89,000	
Property	120,000	
Inventory	4,600	
Payables		6,300
Receivables	5,900	
Bank overdraft		790
Loan		50,000
Capital		100,000
Drawings	23,000	
Sales		330,000
Purchases	165,000	
Sales returns	7,000	
Discounts allowed	3,200	
Sundry expenses	73,890	
Discounts received (β)		4,500
	491,590	491,590

98   B

Where a trial balance agrees, this does not confirm that no errors have been made in the accounting records. Only those errors resulting from a journal entry without an equal debit and credit will be highlighted by the trial balance.

99   C

All three are limitations of a trial balance:

- Figures in the trial balance are not necessarily the final figures to be reported in the financial statements; they are subject to year end adjustments.

- Errors of commission (where an entry has been posted to the wrong account) are not identified by the trial balance since an equal debit and credit entry are still posted.

- Although a trial balance can identify if double entry has broken down, it does not indicate in which accounts wrong entries were made.

100 A

	$	$
Sales		120,000
Opening inventory	2,600	
Purchases	78,900	
Closing inventory	(1,900)	
		(79,600)
Gross profit		40,400
Rental expense (3,400 – 200)	3,200	
Sundry expenses	13,900	
Bank interest	(270)	
Decrease in allowance	(120)	
		(16,710)
Net profit		23,690

101 C

	Dr	Cr
	$	$
Premises	500,000	
Accumulated depreciation		120,000
Inventory	23,000	
Share capital		200,000
Retained profits		105,000
Receivables	43,500	
Carriage in	1,500	
Allowance for receivables		3,400
Bank overdraft		1,010
Payables		35,900
Sales		500,080
Purchases	359,700	
Sales returns	10,300	
Sundry expenses	14,000	
Discounts allowed	1,340	
Suspense	12,050	
	965,390	965,390

102 B

	Increase	Decrease
	$	$
Closing inventory	45,700	
Depreciation (20% × $470,800)		94,160
Irrecoverable debt		230
Deferred income		6,700
	_____	_____
	45,700	101,090
	_____	_____
Decrease in net assets		$55,390

103 C

	Charge for the year				Closing
	$				$
Rent	24,000	Rent accrual			**2,000**
		(12 × $2,000)	Due	24,000	
			Paid	22,000	
				_____	
			Accrual	2,000	
				_____	
Insurance	28,000	Insurance prepayment			**2,000**
			Paid	30,000	
			Due	28,000	
				_____	
			Prepayment	2,000	
				_____	

The rental charge in the statement of profit or loss will be $24,000 ($2,000 × 12 months). Only $22,000 has been paid, therefore an accrual of $2,000 will appear in the statement of financial position. The insurance charge will be according to the notes given after the trial balance totalling $28,000. The amount paid is $30,000, thus a prepayment of $2,000 will appear in the statement of financial position.

Note: In the trial balance the amount paid will be shown.

104 A

	$
Irrecoverable debts 1,600 + 3,000	4,600
Decrease in allowance for receivables (W1)	(440)
Total irrecoverable debt expense	4,160

Receivables (29,600 – 3,000)	26,600
Less: Closing allowance for receivables	(2,660)
Net closing receivables	23,940

(W1)

Closing allowance for receivables [10% × (26,600 – 3,000)]	2,660
Opening allowance for receivables	3,100
Decrease in allowance for receivables	440

105 B

Depreciation charge	= Closing cost × percentage depreciation rate
	= **$5,000** (10% × $50,000)
Closing accumulated depreciation	= Accumulated depreciation b/f + charge for the year
	= $15,000 + $5,000
	= $20,000
Carrying value	= Closing cost less closing accumulated depreciation
Carrying value	=$50,000 – $20,000
	= **$30,000**

106 D

Depreciation charge	= (Closing cost – accumulated depreciation b/f) ×
	percentage depreciation rate
	= ($50,000 – $21,875) × 25%
	= $7,031
Closing accumulated depreciation	= Accumulated depreciation b/f + charge for the year
	= $21,875 + $7,031
	= $ 28,906
Carrying value	= Closing cost less closing accumulated depreciation
Carrying value	= $50,000 – $28,906
Net book value	= $21,094

BOOKS OF PRIME ENTRY AND CONTROL ACCOUNTS

107 C

Day books include:

- Sales day book
- Purchases day book
- Sales returns day book
- Purchases returns day book
- Cash book
- Petty cash book
- The journal

108 B

The imprest amount, or float can always be calculated by adding together the amount in petty cash and the vouchers evidencing expenditure:

$25 + $(7.25 + 12.75 + 15) = $60

109 B

110 C

Receivables ledger control account			
	$		$
Balance b/f	69,472		
Sales	697,104	Cash received	686,912
		Irrecoverable debts	1,697
		Sales returns (β)	3,004
		Balance c/f	74,963
	766,576		766,576

111 A

Opening float	150
Receipts	
Photocopier use	25
Bank	500
Payments	
Cheque cashed	(90)
Payments (β)	385
Closing float	200

112 B

A debit balance on a purchase ledger account means that the business is owed money by its supplier. This could be explained by the company mistakenly paying too much. (For example, a business might pay the full amount of an invoice and then receive a 'credit note' from the supplier for the return of faulty goods.)

113 A

Payables ledger control account

	$		$
Bank	68,900	Balance b/f	34,500
Discounts received	1,200	Purchases (credit)	78,400
Purchase returns	4,700		
Balance c/f	38,100		
	———		———
	112,900		112,900
	———		———
		Balance b/f	38,100

114 B

Receivables ledger control account

	$		$
Sales	250,000	Bank	225,000
Bank: cheque returned	3,500	Sales returns	2,500
		Irrecoverable debts	3,000
		Contra: trade payables	4,000
		Balance c/f	19,000
	———		———
	253,500		253,500
	———		———
Balance b/f	19,000		

115 C

The control account cannot ensure that the personal ledger is free from error. The two totals can agree, but there may be compensating errors in the personal ledger (e.g. the wrong account is debited) or an entry may be missing from both the control account and the ledger.

116 D

A credit entry in the accounts of Y means either that Y owes X $450 or that X owes Y $450 less than before. A credit entry would arise in Y's receivables ledger if customer X returned goods to Y. All the other transactions in the question would result in debit entries.

117 D

The sales day book provides totals for receivables, sales excluding sales tax and tax on the sales. These totals are transferred to the general ledger by debiting the receivables ledger control account with the gross amount receivable, crediting the sales account with the value of sales excluding tax and crediting the sales tax account with the amount of tax payable.

118 B

There is no real point in introducing significant controls to protect an asset worth a maximum of $100 at any given time. Keeping the box locked in a drawer will reduce the risk of it being picked up and stolen without imposing undue inefficiencies or delays in reimbursing valid claims.

119 A

- B describes a purchase order.

- C describes a supplier statement.

- D describes a remittance advice.

120 C

- Quotations are used by a customer to establish the price of goods from various suppliers.

- Goods delivery notes are provided by a supplier to detail goods delivered.

- Debit notes are issued by a customer to cross refer to credit notes issued by a supplier.

- Remittance advice slips are issued by the customer to send to the supplier alongside payment.

- Sales orders are internal documents used by suppliers to record details of orders for goods.

- Purchase orders are sent to suppliers by a customer as a request for supply.

- Purchase invoices are issued by suppliers as a request for payment.

CONTROL ACCOUNT RECONCILIATIONS

121 B

	PLCA		Payables ledger
	$		$
Draft balance	768,420	Draft balance	781,200
Reverse incorrect debit entry	28,400		
Discounts received – correct entry	(15,620)		
	_____		_____
Revised balance	781,200		781,200
	_____		_____

- A and D would explain the discrepancy if the balance on the control account was $12,780 greater than the balance on the payables ledger.

- C would explain the balance on the payables ledger being $25,560 greater than the balance on the control account.

122 A

Payables ledger control account

	$		$
Contras against debit balances in receivables ledger	48,000	Balance b/f	318,600
Cash paid to suppliers	1,364,300	Purchases	1,268,600
Purchase returns	41,200	Refunds received from suppliers	2,700
Discounts received	8,200		
Balance c/f	**128,200**		
	1,589,900		1,589,900

123 D

	Payables ledger	Supplier statement
	$	$
Per question	230	3,980
Cheque (1)		(270)
Goods returned (2)		(180)
Contra (3)		(3,200)
Revised balance	230	330

Difference $100 (330 – 230)

124 A

The control account has been debited by $10 more than it should have been. The account should be credited. This error would have had no effect on the receivables ledger and so part of the difference has been explained.

125 B

	Lord's records
	$
Per question	14,500
Unrecorded discount	(150)
Revised balance = supplier statement	14,350

Lord believes that he owes $150 more than the supplier has stated. Items A, C and D would result in the opposite.

126   D

Items A and B will result in an error in the control account. Item C will result in an error in the total of individual customer account balances. Item D will not affect either of the totals, although there are errors in the individual accounts of the two customers affected, with one account balance too high and the other too low by the same amount.

127   D

	SLCA $
Draft balance per question	37,642
Correction of misposted discount	(1,802)
	————
Revised balance = receivables ledger balance	35,840
	————

The balance on the control account exceeds the total of the individual account balances by $1,802. Items A, B and C would all have the effect of making the total of the individual account balances higher by $1,802. Item D, however, by recording a credit item as a debit item in the control account, has made the control account debit balance too high by $901 × 2 = $1,802.

128   B

	$
Balance per ledger account	260
Cash discount disallowed	80
	———
Adjusted ledger account balance	340
	———

	$
Balance per supplier's statement	1,350
Less: Goods returned	(270)
Cash in transit	(830)
	———
Revised balance	250
	———

Unreconciled difference = ($340 – $250) = $90

129   D

- The purchase day book has been undercast by $500 (i.e. the total is $500 lower than it should be). As a result of this, the purchases account has been debited and the payables ledger control account (total payables) credited with $500 too little.

- The sales day book has been overcast by $700. As a result, the sales account has been credited and the receivables ledger control account (total receivables) has been debited with $700 too much.

- As a result of these errors, the control account balances need to be adjusted, and profit reduced by ($500 + $700) $1,200, by reducing sales and increasing purchases.

- Neither error affects the entries in the accounts of individual customers and suppliers.

130 A

- As a result of the error, total payables are understated by $259,440 − $254,940 = $4,500. To correct the error, increase the balance in the payables ledger control account by crediting the control account.

- The error has affected the control account only, and not the entries in the individual supplier account for Figgins in the purchase ledger, so the total of suppliers' balances is unaffected.

131 B

Error 1. Total sales and total receivables have been recorded $370 too much. Credit the receivables ledger control account by $370.

Error 2. Total receivables has been recorded ($940 − $490) $450 too little. Credit the receivables ledger control account by $450

As a result of these two errors, total receivables have been under-credited by $820 ($450 + $370).

The errors have not affected the accounts of individual customers.

BANK RECONCILIATIONS

132 D

Cash book	$	
Cash book balance per question	(1,350)	Credit therefore overdrawn
Standing order not yet recorded	(300)	
	─────	
Revised cash book balance	(1,650)	
	─────	
	$	
Balance per bank statement (β)	(1,707)	debit
Unpresented cheques	(56)	
Uncleared lodgements	128	
Bank error	(15)	
	─────	
Revised balance = cash book balance	(1,650)	
	─────	

On the bank statement the overdrawn balance is shown as a debit (i.e. from the bank's perspective they are owed money)

133 B

Note that the draft ledger account balance shows an overdraft, however the bank statement shows a positive balance:

	Bank statement $	Ledger account $
Balance per question	250	(190)
Unpresented cheques	(150)	
Misposting of cash receipt		260
Bank interest		30
	100	100

134 C

1   Unpresented cheques are those issued by a business but not yet banked by the recipient. They should be deducted from the balance shown on the bank statement in order to reflect the true bank balance.

2   A dishonoured cheque is recorded by crediting the cash book. The cheque would previously have been debited to cash when received. The credit is the reversal of that entry.

3   A bank error should be corrected by amendment to the balance per the bank statement.

4   From the bank's perspective an overdraft means that they are owed money by the customer. Hence it is shown as a debit (an asset to the bank) in the bank statement.

135 B

	$
Balance per bank statement (overdrawn)	(38,640)
Add: Lodgement not credited	19,270
	(19,370)
Less: Unpresented cheques	(14,260)
Balance per cash book	(33,630)

136 B

	$
Balance per bank statement	(200)
Unpresented cheques	(1,250)
Error	97
Uncleared lodgements	890
Revised balance = revised cash book balance	(463)

KAPLAN PUBLISHING

137 B

	$
Cash book balance	(8,970)
Bank charges	(550)
Revised cash book balance	(9,520)
Bank statement balance (β)	(11,200)
Unpresented cheques	(3,275)
Uncleared lodgements	5,380
Bank error	(425)
Revised cash book balance	(9,520)

138 B

Cash

	$		$
Original balance (β)	11,960		
Error: receipt recorded as payment (2 × $195)	390	Dishonoured cheque	300
		Bank charges	50
		Balance c/f (= revised bank balance)	12,000
	12,350		12,350

	$
Bank statement balance	13,400
Unpresented cheques	(1,400)
Revised balance	12,000

139 D

	$
Balance per bank statement	(715)
Less: Unpresented cheques	(824)
	(1,539)
Add: Outstanding lodgements	337
	(1,202)
Less: Bank error	(25)
Statement of financial position/cash book overdraft	(1,227)

140 D

Cash

	$		$
		Draft balance	5,675
Reversal of standing order (entered twice)	125	Dishonoured cheque	900
Revised balance	6,450		
	6,575		6,575

Note: The dishonoured cheque for $450 should have been credited to the bank balance. Instead it was debited. The bank balance is therefore too high by $900.

141 B

Cash book

	$		$
Cash sales	1,450	Balance b/f	485
Cash receipts	2,400	Payments to suppliers (95% × $1,800)	1,710
		Dishonoured cheques	250
		Balance c/f	1,405
	3,850		3,850

142 B

	$
Balance per bank statement	(800)
Unpresented cheque	(80)
Revised bank balance	(880)

The dishonoured cheque requires adjustment in the cash book. After this adjustment, the cash book balance will equal the revised bank balance.

143 B

Cash

	$		$
Draft balance	2,490		
		Bank charges	50
		Dishonoured cheque	140
		Revised balance	2,300
	2,490		2,490

144 A

Cash

	$		$
		Draft balance	1,240
		Bank charges	75
Revised balance	1,315		
	1,315		1,315

	$
Balance per bank statement (β)	(1,005)
Unpresented cheques	(450)
Uncleared lodgements	140
Revised balance = cash book balance	(1,315)

145 C

An unrecorded difference is a transaction that is reflected in the bank statement but has not yet been entered into the cash book – usually because the accountant is not aware of the transaction until advised by the bank.

Examples include direct debits, standing orders, bank charges, bank interest, dishonoured cheques and direct credits. Uncleared lodgements and unpresented cheques are examples of timing differences – amounts which have been entered into the cash book but have not yet cleared the bank.

CORRECTION OF ERRORS AND SUSPENSE ACCOUNTS

146 A

Suspense account

	$		$
Imbalance on TB (362,350 – 347,800)	14,550		
Disposals (2)	9,000		
Allowance for receivables (3)	2,600	Balance c/f	26,150
	_____		_____
	26,150		26,150
	_____		_____
Balance b/f	26,150		

The suspense account is only affected where the initial debit and credit were unequal:

1   An incorrect entry into the sales day book means that the subtotal of the day book is wrong and both sides of the double entry have been made for the wrong amount. This does not affect the suspense account.

2   An unequal entry has occurred:

		$
Entry was:	Dr Cash	9,000
	(Cr Suspense	9,000)
To correct:	Dr Suspense	9,000
	Cr Disposals	9,000

(Do not worry about the other journals required to record the disposal – they have not been recorded at all and so do not affect the suspense account.)

3   An unequal entry has occurred:

		$
Entry was:	Dr Irrecoverable debt expense	1,300
	Dr Allowance for receivables	1,300
	(Cr Suspense	2,600)
To correct:	Dr Suspense	2,600
	Cr Allowance for receivables	2,600

147 C

- If the sales day book is undercast, then the debit and credit entries to the accounts are equal (although for the wrong amount).

- Discounts allowed should be debited to the discounts allowed account. The debit entry has simply been made to the wrong account. It is assumed that the credit entry is correct and therefore an equal debit and credit entry have been made.

- The omission of an opening accrual or prepayment will always result in an imbalance on the trial balance.

- The undercasting of the debit side of the cash account will result in an incorrect balance for cash being extracted and shown on the trial balance. This will cause total debit balances to be unequal to total credit balances.

148 A

- An extraction error arises when the balance on a particular account is not listed correctly in the trial balance. Therefore the trial balance does not balance.

- An error of commission arises where an equal debit and credit have been recorded but one entry has been made to the wrong account.

- An error of omission arises where a transaction has been completely omitted from the accounting records.

- An error of original entry arises where an equal debit and credit have been made but for the wrong amount.

149 D

- The suspense account initially has a credit balance in order to make the total debits equal to the total credits.

- Where an opening accrual has been omitted, it should be recorded and the opposite entry made to the suspense account:

Dr Suspense account $7,568
Cr Rental expense $7,568

Suspense account

	$		$
Opening accrual	7,568	Per trial balance	7,568

Tutorial note:

Discounts allowed should be a debit in the trial balance of $3,784. If the account balance is wrongly shown as a credit, the total credits in the trial balance will exceed the total debits by 2 × $3,784.

Discounts received

Correct entry		*Actual entry*	
Dr Payables ledger control account	$3,784	Cr Payables ledger control account	$3,784
Cr Discounts received.	$3,784	Cr Discounts received	$3,784
		(Dr Suspense account	$7,568

The actual entry made was a double credit. This will result in a debit balance arising on the suspense account.

Sales day book

If the sales day book is undercast, the entries to the sales and receivables ledger control accounts will be equal, but for the wrong amount. This will not result in an imbalance on the trial balance.

150 C

- The correct entry for discounts allowed is:

Dr Discounts allowed

Cr Receivables ledger control account (receivables)

- As the debit was made to the discounts received account in error, the amount needs reversing out of the discounts received account by way of a credit.

- The correct debit should then be posted to the discounts allowed account.

Note:

- Personal accounts are not maintained for the directors of a company

- Where repairs are carried out by a company's own staff using items of inventory , the correct journal to transfer the relevant costs to the repairs account is:

Dr Repairs

Cr Wages/purchases

If rent received is credited to the wrong account, no suspense account entry arises. The correction journal will involve debiting the account wrongly credited and crediting the rent receivable account.

151 B

1   A debit and credit are made for an equal amount (albeit to the wrong account in the case of the debit), and therefore the suspense account is not affected.

2   The undercasting of the debit side of the wages account will result in an incorrect balance being extracted. This will result in an imbalance on the trial balance and the creation of a suspense account.

3   The correct entry for discounts allowed is:

Dr Discounts allowed

Cr Receivables ledger control account (receivables)

The error made will therefore result in a double credit (correctly to the receivables ledger control account, and incorrectly to discounts received). Where double entry breaks down, a suspense account will be created.

4   An equal debit and credit entry are made and therefore the suspense account is not affected.

152 C

Should do		Did do		To correct	
Dr Discounts allowed	13,000	Cr Discounts received	13,000	Dr Discounts received	13,000
Cr SLCA (receivables)	13,000	Cr SLCA (receivables)	13,000	Dr Discounts allowed	13,000
		(Dr Suspense	26,000)	Cr Suspense	13,000
Dr Plant and machinery	18,000	(Dr Suspense	18,000)	Dr Plant and machinery	18,000
Cr Cash	18,000	Cr Cash	18,000	Cr Suspense	18,000

153 B

1   Double entry has been maintained (an equal debit and credit entry have been made). Therefore there is no effect on the suspense account.

To correct:
Dr Plant account		$43,200
Cr Cash		$43,200

In addition, depreciation should have been charged at 10% × $48,000, i.e. $4,800.

To record extra depreciation:
Dr Depreciation expense	$4,320
Cr Accumulated depreciation	$4,320

2   This transaction has been omitted completely from the accounts therefore it has no effect on the suspense account.

To correct:
Dr Bank charges		$440
Cr Cash		$440

3   A debit entry has been made, but no credit entry. A suspense account entry will therefore be required to correct this error:

Should do		*Did do*		*To correct*	
Dr Payables ledger account	$800	Dr Payables ledger account	$800	Dr Suspense	$800
Cr Sundry payables (amount due to Director)	$800	(Cr suspense	$800)	Cr Sundry payables	$800

4   The balance on the cash book will be $10,000 too high as a result of the understatement. Therefore the trial balance will not balance and a suspense account will arise.

To correct:
Dr Suspense	$10,000
Cr Cash	$10,000

154 D

Correction journals only affect profit if one side is posted to an statement of profit or loss account and the other to a statement of financial position account. For this purpose, a suspense account is a statement of financial position account:

	Increase	*Decrease*	
	$	$	$
Draft profit			630,000
1 Extra depreciation		4,320	
2 Bank charges		440	
3 No effect			
4 No effect			
			(4,760)
			625,240

155 C

Profit is only affected when one (but not both) side of the correction journal is posted to the statement of profit or loss.

- Both entries in the journal to record cash drawings are to statement of financial position accounts.

- The expense of $420 has already been recorded when the allowance was made during the year.

- To correct the misclassification, interest receivable will be reduced and rental income increased by the same amount. Therefore there is no effect on profit.

- Both entries in the journal to record the receipt are to statement of financial position accounts.

156 C

Should do		Did do		To correct	
Dr Purchases	$4,000	Dr Purchases	$4,700	Dr Suspense	$700
Dr Sales tax	$700	Dr Sales tax	$700	Cr Purchases	$700
Cr PLCA	$4,700	Cr PLCA	$4,700		
		(Cr Suspense	$700)		

- Purchases (and sales) are recorded net of sales tax.

- Payables (and receivables) are recorded gross of sales tax.

157 A

Suspense account

	$		$
Balance per TB	500	Misrecording of decrease in allowance for receivables	840
Sales account undercast	150		
Balance c/f	190		–
	840		840
		Balance b/f	190

- The misposting of rent received to the rent payable account does not affect the suspense account as double entry was maintained, despite the error.

158 C

An error of principle breaks the 'rules' of an accounting principle or concept, for example incorrectly treating revenue expenditure as capital expenditure. The purchase of a non-current asset should be debited to a non-current asset account, not to the purchases account.

159 B

Should do		Did do		To correct	
1 Dr Motor expense	$4,600	Cr Cash	$4,600	Dr Motor expense	$4,600
Cr Cash	$4,600	Cr MV cost	$4,600	Dr MV cost	$4,600
		(Dr Suspense	$9,200)	Cr Suspense	$9,200
2 Dr Cash	$360	Dr Cash	$360	Dr Green's account	$360
Cr Brown's account	$360	Cr Green's account	$360	Cr Brown's account	$360
3 Dr Rent expense	$9,500	Dr Rent expense	$5,900	Dr Rent expense	$3,600
Cr Cash	$9,500	Cr Cash	$9,500	Cr Suspense	$3,600
		(Dr Suspense	$3,600)		
4 Dr Discounts allowed		Dr Discounts received		Dr Discounts allowed	
Cr SLCA		Cr SLCA		Cr Discounts received	
5 Dr Cash	$100	–		Dr Cash	$100
Cr Sales	$100			Cr Sales	$100

160 B

By crediting $40 to the Discounts Allowed account, when the discount should have been debited to the account, discounts allowed have been reduced by $40 when they should have been increased by $40. As a result of this error, profit has been overstated by 2 × $40 = $80.

161 A

Should do	Did do	To correct
1 Dr Gas expense $420	Dr Gas expense $240	Dr Gas expense $180
Cr Cash $420	Cr Cash $420	Cr Suspense $180
	(Dr Suspense $180)	
2 Dr Discounts allowed $50	Cr Discounts received $50	Dr Discounts allowed $50
Cr SLCA $50	Cr SLCA $50	Dr Discounts received $50
	(Dr Suspense $100)	Cr Suspense $100
3 Dr Bank $70	Dr Bank $70	Dr Suspense $70
Cr Interest $70	(Cr Suspense $70)	Cr Interest $70

Suspense account

	$		$
Balance b/f (β)	210	Error 1	180
Error 3	70	Error 2	100
	———		———
	280		280
	———		———

162 D

The error has been to debit the customer (receivable) account and credit the supplier (payable) account, instead of debiting the supplier account and crediting the customer account. As a result receivables are over-stated by 2 × $270 = $540, and payables are over-stated by $540. The error should be corrected, but sales and purchases are unaffected, so profit is unaffected. Total assets (receivables) and total liabilities (payables) are both $540 too high, so that net assets are unchanged.

INCOMPLETE RECORDS

163 A

	$	$	%
Sales		650,000	100
Cost of sales			
Opening inventory	380,000		
Purchases	480,000		
Lost inventory (β)	**(185,000)**		
Closing inventory	(220,000)		
		(455,000)	70
Gross profit		195,000	30

164 D

	$	$	%
Sales (100/70 × $756,000)		**1,080,000**	100
Cost of sales			
Opening Inventory	77,000		
Purchases	763,000		
Closing Inventory	(84,000)		
		(756,000)	70
		324,000	30

165 B

	$	$	%
Sales (174,825 – 1,146)		173,679	125%
Cost of goods sold			
Opening inventory	12,274		
Purchases (136,527 – 1,084)	135,443		
Closing inventory (β)	**(8,774)**		
	‾‾‾‾‾‾		
$173,679 × 100/125		(138,943)	100%
		‾‾‾‾‾‾	
Gross profit		34,736	25%

166 D

	$	$	%
Sales		630,000	140
Cost of sales			
Opening Inventory	24,300		
Purchases (β)	458,450		
Closing Inventory	(32,750)		
	‾‾‾‾‾‾		
100/140 × $630,000		(450,000)	100
		‾‾‾‾‾‾	
		180,000	40

Payables ledger control account

	$		$
		Balance b/f	29,780
Cash paid to suppliers (β)	**453,630**	Purchases (cash and credit)	458,450
Balance c/f	34,600		
	‾‾‾‾‾‾		‾‾‾‾‾‾
	488,230		488,230
	‾‾‾‾‾‾		‾‾‾‾‾‾

167 C

	$
Inventory at 6 January 20X6	32,780
Sales at cost (β)	6,020
Purchases	(4,200)
	‾‾‾‾‾‾
Inventory at 31 December 20X5	34,600

Profit on sales: $8,600 – $6,020 = $2,580

Gross margin: $\dfrac{2,580}{8,600} = 30\%$

168 D

Cash

	$		$
Balance b/f	620		
Receipts from customers (β)	16,660	Payments	16,780
		Balance c/f	500
	_____		_____
	17,280		17,280
	_____		_____

Receivables

	$		$
Balance b/f	6,340		
Sales (β)	15,520	Cash receipts	16,660
		Balance c/f	5,200
	_____		_____
	21,860		21,860
	_____		_____

Gross profit: 25/125 × $15,520 = $3,104

169 B

	$	$
Sales		148,000
Opening inventory	34,000	
Purchases	100,000	
	_____	
	134,000	
Closing inventory (β)	**(26,000)**	
	_____	
Cost of sales (148,000 – 40,000)		108,000
		_____
Gross profit		40,000
		_____

170 C

You might need to answer this by testing each answer in turn.

$$\frac{\text{Gross profit}}{\text{Cost of sales}} \quad \frac{28,800}{72,000} = 40\%$$

	$
Sales	100,800
Cost of sales	(72,000)
	_____
Gross profit	28,800
	_____

171 D

Trade payables

	$		$
Cash paid	542,300	Balance b/f	142,600
Discounts received	13,200		
Goods returned	27,500		
Balance c/f	137,800	Purchases (β)	**578,200**
	720,800		720,800

172 D

Trade receivables

	$		$
Balance b/f	10,000	Receipts from sales	85,000
Sales (β)	**84,000**		
		Balance c/f	9,000
	94,000		94,000

173 C

Cash

	$		$
Balance b/f	300	Bankings	50,000
Proceeds of sale of car	5,000	Wages	12,000
Sales (β)	**81,100**	Drawings	24,000
		Balance c/f	400
	86,400		86,400

174 C

	$	$	%
Sales		480,000	150
Cost of sales			
Opening inventory	36,420		
Purchases (β)	324,260		
Closing inventory	(40,680)		
100/150 × $480,000		(320,000)	100
		180,000	50

PLCA

	$		$
		Balance b/f	29,590
Cash paid (β)	**319,975**	Purchases	324,260
Balance c/f	33,875		
	─────		─────
	353,850		353,850
	─────		─────

175 B

Closing net assets	=	Opening net assets	+	Capital injections	–	Loss for the period	–	Drawings
($56,000 – $18,750)		($40,000 – $14,600)						($6,800 + $250)
$37,250	=	$25,400	+	$20,000	–	(β) **$1,100**	–	$7,050

176 D

- As the inventory is insured, its cost (not selling price) is recoverable from the insurer. Therefore this amount is shown as a current asset.

- The cost should also be taken out of cost of sales as these goods have not been sold.

COMPANY ACCOUNTS

177 C

	Cost of sales	Administrative expense	Distribution costs
	$	$	$
Opening inventory	12,500		
Closing inventory	(17,900)		
Purchases	199,000		
Distribution costs			35,600
Administrative expenses		78,800	
Audit fee		15,200	
Carriage in	3,500		
Carriage out			7,700
Depreciation (70:30:0)	28,000	12,000	
	─────	─────	─────
	225,100	106,000	43,300
	─────	─────	─────

178 B

- The first statement is false: the nominal value of the ordinary shares is 50c and therefore there are 200,000 in issue. The ordinary dividend paid is:

  200,000 × 3c = $6,000

- The second statement is true. A preference dividend is accounted for when it falls due and therefore the part of the dividend not yet paid must be accrued at the year end.

179 C

Share premium

	$		$
		Balance b/f	30,000
Bonus issue (W2)	12,500	Rights issue (W1)	90,000
Balance c/f	107,500		
	120,000		120,000

(W1)	**Rights issue**	Existing number of shares	400,000
		New shares	100,000
	At $1.15 each	Dr Cash	$115,000
		Cr Share capital	$25,000
		Cr Share premium	$90,000
(W2)	**Bonus issue**	Existing shares	500,000
		New shares	50,000
		Dr Share premium	$12,500
		Cr Share capital	$12,500

180 D

- Only dividend income is shown in the statement of profit or loss and other comprehensive income.

- Only dividends payable in respect of preference shares are shown in the statement of financial position.

- The statement of cash flows includes all dividends paid.

- The statement of changes in equity includes dividends paid and dividends payable.

181 C

- The tax charge is disclosed in the statement of profit or loss and other comprehensive income.

- A revaluation surplus is not realised. However, under IAS 1 (revised) it is included in the statement of profit or loss and other comprehensive income and also shown in the statement of changes in equity.

182 D

- Dividends are not shown in a company's statement of profit or loss and other comprehensive income. Instead they are presented in the statement of changes to equity.

- Unpaid ordinary dividends are only accrued at the year end if they have been declared prior to the year end. In practise this is very rare.

183 A

- A rights issue involves the issue of new shares for cash and therefore more equity capital will be raised.

- The rights issue price will probably be above nominal value and therefore the share premium account will be increased by the amount of the premium. A bonus issue does not involve cash; when recording the transaction, the debit entry is normally made to the share premium account, therefore reducing it.

- Both a rights and a bonus issue involve the potential issue of shares to existing shareholders. Therefore neither will increase the number of shareholders in a company.

- A bonus issue will result in more shares in issue without affecting the value of the company as a whole. Therefore each share will be worth less, not more.

184 C

- An overprovision from a previous year reduces the tax charge to the statement of profit or loss and other comprehensive income.

- Tax payable is the full amount of the estimation of the charge for the year.

185 C

- The credit sale is part of the company's normal operating cycle and is therefore classified as a current asset.

- The bank overdraft is repayable on demand and so classified as a current liability.

- The shares have been purchased to sell and so are classified as a current asset investment.

186 D

	Share capital $	Share premium $	Revaluation reserve $	Retained earnings $	Total $
Share issue	2,000	3,000			5,000
Revaluation			230,000		230,000
Profit (178,000 – 45,000 – 5,600)				127,400	127,400
Dividends – ordinary				(12,000)	(12,000)
– preference				(8,000)	(8,000)
Total change	2,000	3,000	230,000	107,400	342,400

187 D

- Preference shares do not generally carry voting rights.

- Preference dividends are fixed amounts, normally expressed as a percentage of their nominal value.

- Preference dividends are paid out in preference to ordinary dividends.

188 A

- Accounting standards require that the commercial substance of a transaction is recorded rather than its legal form.

- Redeemable preference shares are repayable at a specified future date and therefore have the qualities of debt.

- They are therefore accounted for as liabilities.

189 B

- Paid up share capital is the amount of the nominal value which have been paid currently.

- Issued share capital is the share capital which has actually been issued to shareholders.

- Authorised share capital is the nominal value of the maximum number of shares that a company can have in issue at any one time.

190 B

- Loan notes can be issued at a discount to their nominal value (unlike shares).

- Interest is always paid based on the nominal value.

- Interest accrued $8,000 (12% × $400,000 × 2/12)

191 A

- A bonus share issue does not raise finance for a company, as the shares are issued for no consideration (i.e. for free).

- Each share becomes worth less (as there are more shares in issue but the value of the company as a whole remains the same), and so more marketable.

- The reserves decreases when there is a bonus issue. The double entry is to debit the reserves and credit the share capital.

- Share capital increases (at the expense of other reserves) and so may seem more appropriate when compared to net assets.

192 D

Transfers between revenue reserves, as mentioned in A and B, have no effect on the overall total of revenue reserves; issuing shares at a premium increases capital reserves; the paying of dividends must be from revenue reserves, so these will decrease.

ACCOUNTING STANDARDS

193 C

- A flood does not provide additional information to conditions existing at the year end and therefore is non-adjusting.

- The credit customer's bankruptcy occurs after the accounts are approved.

- The declaration of an ordinary dividend is a non-adjusting event.

194 A

- The refund policy creates a constructive obligation.

- Provision should be made for the best estimate of the value of refunds. This may be based on expected values.

- The legal claim is only possible, therefore the company cannot provide for the loss; instead they should disclose details of the case.

195 B

196 A

- Intangible assets may be internally generated or purchased.

- They are often used to generate profits in the long term.

- Their key characteristic is their lack of physical substance.

197 A

198 D

- Details of adjusting events are not disclosed by note; instead the event is accounted for.

- The sale of inventory after the reporting date at a price lower than that at which it is valued in the statement of financial position is an adjusting event.

- A fall in the market value of investments after the reporting date is a non-adjusting event. It should therefore be disclosed if material.

199 A

- Warranties meet the criteria required to create a provision; a provision should be made for the best estimate of the obligation.

- The likelihood of a liability arising for Quidditch as a result of the guarantee is assessed as possible. A provision cannot be recorded unless the likelihood is probable.

200 C

The costs of a development project are capitalised only if:

- The project is separately identifiable.

- Expenditure can be reliably measured.

- It is commercially viable.

- It is technically feasible.

- It is projected to be profitable.

- Resources are available to complete it.

- Project 2 falls short of these criteria: it does not appear that the appetite suppressant properties of the substance have yet been confirmed and therefore it is not yet commercially viable.

- Project 3 may not be completed and therefore does not meet all six criteria.

- The costs of projects 2 and 3 should be expensed to the statement of profit or loss and other comprehensive income.

201 A

	$
Project A	34,000
Project B	78,870
Project C ($290,000 + $19,800) × 4/36	34,422
	——————
	147,292
	——————

- Project A is a research project and all costs should be written off to the statement of profit or loss and other comprehensive income as incurred.

- Project B is a development project. Costs can only be capitalised once the capitalisation criteria are met. Those costs incurred before this was the case cannot be reinstated as an asset.

- Project C is a development project which has resulted in capitalised expenditure. This asset must be amortised over the 36 months of sales of the product. Amortisation for the current year should be 4 months (1 September to 31 December 20X5).

202 B

- 1 is a change in accounting estimate and should be accounted for prospectively (i.e. the change should be applied going forward, but previous periods' figures should not be revised).

- 2 is a change in accounting policy and should be accounted for retrospectively (i.e. opening reserves are adjusted to show the position as if the new policy had always been in place).

203 B

- Revenue should not be recognised on the first transaction until the specialist installation is complete.

- The second transaction is a normal credit sale and revenue should be recognised regardless of the fact that cash has not yet been received.

204 A

STATEMENT OF CASH FLOWS

205 D

	$
Issue of shares (560,000 – 220,000)	340,000
Issue of loan notes	300,000
	640,000

- Interest paid is included within the 'operating activities' heading of the cash flow statement.

206 B

- Interest received = $13,000.

- Interest and dividends paid are normally shown within cash from operating activities. An alternative presentation may place them within cash from financing activities.

207 C

- Bonus issues do not involve the transfer of cash, whereas rights issues result in a cash inflow.

- The revaluation of non-current assets does not involve the transfer of cash.

208 D

- Depreciation is a non-cash expense and should therefore be added back to profit.

- An increase in assets (inventory and receivables) means that less cash is available (as it has been used to fund assets), hence an increase in assets is shown as a deduction in the cash flow statement.

- An increase in liabilities (payables) means that more cash is available (i.e. it has not been used to pay liabilities), hence an increase in liabilities is shown as an addition in the cash flow statement.

209 D

- The carrying value of non-current assets is shown in the statement of financial position.

- Depreciation charged on non-current assets and any profit or loss on disposal is shown in the statement of profit or loss and other comprehensive income.

- Revaluation surpluses relating to non-current assets are shown in the statement of changes in equity.

- In relation to non-current assets, the indirect statement of cash flows will include:
  - depreciation
  - profit or loss on disposal
  - proceeds of the disposal of non-current assets
  - payments to acquire non-current assets.

210 D

	$	
Cash generated from operations (β)	419,254	
Tax and dividends paid	(87,566)	
	————	
Net cash from operating activities (β)		331,688
Purchase of property, plant and equipment	(47,999)	
Proceeds from sale of property, plant and equipment	13,100	
	————	
Net cash from investing activities		(34,899)
Redemption of loans	(300,000)	
	————	
Net cash from financing activities		(300,000)
		————
Decrease in cash and cash equivalents		(3,211)
		————

211 A

	$000
Profit for the year (β)	**1,175**
Add back depreciation	100
Less: Increase in receivables & inventory	(575)
	————
Cash flow from operating activities	700
Add: Cash from issue of shares	1,000
Less: Repayment of debentures	(750)
Less: Purchase of non-current assets	(200)
	————
Increase in cash	750
	————

212   B

Non-current assets book value

	$		$
Balance b/f	50,000	Disposals (4,000 – 1,500)	2,500
Additions (β)	7,500	Depreciation	9,000
		Balance c//f	46,000
	_____		_____
	57,500		57,500
	_____		_____

213   C

	$
Profit	8,000
Add: Depreciation (not a cash expense)	12,000
	_____
	20,000
Purchase of new non-current assets	(25,000)
	_____
Fall in cash balance	(5,000)
	_____

214   D

	$000
Profit for the year	18,750
Depreciation	1,250
Non-current asset purchases	(8,000)
Decrease in inventories	1,800
Increase in receivables	(1,000)
Increase in payables	350
	_____
Increase in cash and cash equivalents	13,150
	_____

215   D

Items added include the depreciation charge for the period, any losses on disposals of non-current assets, reductions in inventories and receivables (including prepayments) and any increase in trade payables (including accruals).

216 D

Statement 1 is incorrect: net cash flow from operating activities is the same, whichever method of presentation is used.

Statement 2 is incorrect. Companies with high profits can be cash-negative, due to high spending on new non-current assets and/or a large build-up of working capital.

Statement 3 is incorrect. Profits and losses on non-current asset disposals are shown as an adjustment to net profit before tax.

217 D

- New purchase (additions) are given in the question as $2,000.

- The assets disposed of had a cost of $3,000 and accumulated depreciation at the time of disposal of $1,500. Their carrying value at disposal was therefore $1,500. The profit on disposal was $500, so the cash received from the disposal was $2,000.

218 A

Major non-cash transactions are not highlighted within the statement of cash flows (although they are disclosed elsewhere in a set of accounts). These are of interest to the users of accounts as they may have an impact on future cash flows.

219 D

	$
Cash sales	212,500
Less:	
Cash purchases	(1,600)
Cash expenses	(11,200)
Cash paid to credit suppliers (W1)	(121,780)
Cash paid as wages and salaries (W2)	(33,800)
Cash generated from operations	41,120

(W1)

Payables

	$		$
		Balance b/f	12,300
Cash paid (β)	121,780	Purchases	123,780
Balance c/f	14,300		
	136,080		136,080

(W2)

Wages and salaries

	$		$
		Balance b/f	1,500
Cash paid (β)	33,800	Statement of profit or loss and other comprehensive income expense	34,600
Balance c/f	2,300		
	─────		─────
	36,100		36,100
	─────		─────

220 C

	$000
Retained profit for the year ($82,000 – $72,000)	10,000
Add back:	
Dividends payable (current year's)	1,600
Tax payable (current year's estimate)	15,000
Loan note interest payable (10% × $40,000)	4,000
	─────
Operating profit	30,600
	─────

The additional $10,000 loan notes were issued at the beginning of the year. Therefore, the total loan notes at the start of the year will be $40,000. The loan notes interest for the year will be $4,000 (i.e. 10% × $40,000).

REGULATORY FRAMEWORK

221 A

222 C

223 A

Accounting standards provide guidance on common transactions. They cannot provide guidance on all types of transactions.

224 D

- If applicable, the going concern concept presumes that a business will continue in operational existence for the foreseeable future.

- Commercial substance should always be reflected in financial statements, even where this differs from legal form.

- A revaluation surplus is not realised however, it is credited the statement of profit or loss and other comprehensive income and then shown in the statement of changes in equity.

225 A

226 D

The replacement cost of an asset is often referred to as its current cost.

227 D

If a business is a going concern, it is reasonable to assume that non-current assets will be used over their expected useful economic life. It is therefore appropriate to value a non-current asset at cost less accumulated depreciation, which represents the consumption of value so far.

228 B

229 D

Information that is faithfully represented may take longer to obtain and verify. Therefore the information may be provided to users on a less timely basis.

230 B

231 B

The historical cost concept is to value assets and liabilities at their original cost to the business, and so fails to take account of changing price levels over time. This is a particular problem with assets that are held for a long time and tend to rise in value, particularly land and buildings. However, the historical cost concept does have regard to depreciation of non-current assets and loss in value, so answer C is incorrect.

232 D

Falling prices (deflation) are not usual. If deflation does occur, historical cost accounting will overstate the current value of assets in the statement of financial position. Profits will be understated. Perhaps the easiest way to think about this is that if assets are valued at historical cost when their current value is much lower due to deflation, depreciation charges will be higher and profit lower.

233 C

234 B

The Framework is not an accounting standard itself, although it is used as a basis when new standards are produced.

235 A

- Historical cost accounting maintains financial capital but not physical capital.

- It does not result in the statement of financial position giving an accurate valuation of the business.

GROUP FINANCIAL STATEMENTS

236 A

	$
Cost of investment	1,400,000
FV of NCI @ acquisition	525,000
Less fair value of net assets at acquisition –	
$(600,000 \times 0.50) + \$50,000$	(350,000)
	————
	1,575,000
	————

237 C

	$
Reserves of Tom	400,000
Post acquisition reserves of Jerry –	
$(\$20,000 \times 80\%)$	16,000
	————
	416,000
	————

238 C

	$
Cost of investment	750,000
FV of NCI @ acquisition	150,000
Less fair value of net assets at acquisition –	
$\$20,000 + \$10,000$	(30,000)
	————
Goodwill	870,000
	————

239 B

	$
FV of NCI @ acquisition	25,000
Post acquisition reserves of Barlow	2,000
(15,000 – 10,000) × 40%	
	27,000

240 A

	$
FV of NCI @ acquisition	50,000
Post acquisition reserves of Barlow	5,250
(75,000 – 60,000) × 35%	
	55,250

241 A

Receivables = 540 + 160 – 40 =	$660,000
Payables = 320 + 180 – 40 =	$460,000

242 B

	$	
Sales value	1,044	120%
Cost value	870	100%
Profit	174	20%

Workings:

Mark up means profit is based on cost, therefore cost represents 100%. If profit is 20%, the sales value must be worth 120%.

Total profit is $174 and 60% is still in stock = $104.40

243 B

Non-current assets = $1,800,000 + $2,200,000 + fair value adj 400,000 = $4,400,000

244 C

	$m	
Sales value	24	100%
Cost value	18	75%
Total profit	6	25%

Workings:

Profit is $6m and half of the amount is still in inventory i.e. $3m

245 D

Sales = 120 + 48 − 24 (inter-company) = $144m

Cost of sales = 84 + 40 − 24 + 3 (PUP) = $103m

246 A

Profit attributable to non-controlling interest should be $6,000,000 × 20% = $1,200,000

The PURP adjustment does not affect the NCI as the parent is selling to the subsidiary.

247 A

Non-current assets = 1,918,000 + 1,960,000 = 3,878,000

Note: We do not include the associates assets and liabilities in the consolidated statement of financial position.

248 B

	$
Reserves of Really	2,464,000
Post acquisition reserves –	
($1,204,000 + $112,000)) × 75%	987,000
($896,000 − $280,000) × 30%	184,800
	3,635,800

249 C

Ownership of more than 50% of the ordinary shares of another company indicates a control relationship – such investments should be accounted for as a subsidiary. Ownership of less than 20% of the ordinary shares of another company is not normally enough to indicate either significant influence or control relationships: such a shareholding should be accounted for as a trade investment.

 KAPLAN PUBLISHING

250   D

The necessary elements to determine whether a control relationship exists between two companies is that one company has power over the other, that it has exposure or rights to variable returns from the other company and that it is able to use power over the other company to affect the returns (i.e. dividends) that it receives from that investment. The ability to exercise significant influence relates to an investment classified as an associate.

INTERPRETATION OF FINANCIAL STATEMENTS

251   D

$(4,600 / 20,000) \times 100 = 23\%$

252   A

20X5 $(2,140/20,000) \times 100 = 10.7\%$

20X6 $(2,180/26,000) \times 100 = 8.38\%$

253   A

20X5 $(4,400 / 20,000) \times 365 = 80$ days

20X6 $(6,740 / 26,000) \times 365 = 95$ days

254   A

$12,715 / 50 = 254$

255   C

		$
Selling price (SP)	140	700
Cost of sales (COS)	100	???
		————
Gross profit	40	???
		————

Cost of sales $\times 140/100 = 700$ Cost of sales $= 700/1.4 = \$ 500$

256 D

Rate of inventories turnover is found by dividing cost of goods sold by average inventory.

Average inventory is

$$\left(\frac{24,000 + 20,000}{2} \right) = \$22,000$$

$$\text{Inventory turnover} = \frac{\text{Cost of sales}}{\text{Average inventory}}$$

	$
Opening inventory	24,000
Purchases	160,000
	————
	184,000
Less: Closing inventory	(20,000)
	————
Cost of goods sold	164,000
	————

Rate of inventory turnover is therefore 164,000/22,000 – 7.45 times

257 D

You need only know the correct formula here.

258 C

The current ratio is current assets: current liabilities, that is 5,800:2,200 = 2.6:1

259 A

The gearing ratio is the proportion of long-term loans to shareholders' funds, thus it follows that if a decrease in long-term loans is less than a decrease in the shareholders' funds, the gearing ratio will rise.

260 B

The quick ratio is current assets minus inventory: current liabilities, that is 2,000:2,200 = 0.9:1.

Section 4

ANSWERS TO MULTI-TASK QUESTIONS

1   ICE

Statement of profit or loss for year ended 31 December 20X1

	$
Revenue ($600,000 – $500 (W1))	599,500
Cost of sales (W2)	(255,000)
Gross profit	344,599
Administrative expenses (W3)	(236,000)
Distribution costs	(75,000)
Operating profit	33,500
Finance costs ($100,000 × 6% × 9/12)	(4,500)
Profit before tax	29,000
Income tax expense	(6,000)
Profit after taxation	23,000

Statement of financial position as at 31 December 20X1

	$
Non- current assets	
Property, plant and equipment	84,000
($120,000 – $15,000 – $21,000 (W2))	
Current assets	
Inventories	30,000
Receivables (W4)	17,000
Cash and cash equivalents	130,000
Total assets	261,000

EQUITY AND LIABILITIES	$
Equity	
Ordinary share capital	5,000
Retained earnings ($43,500 + $23,000 (P/L)	66,500
Non-current liabilities	
Loan	100,000
Current liabilities	
Trade and other payables ($29,000 + $4,500 loan interest)	33,500
Tax payable	6,000
Provision	50,000
	———
Total equity and liabilities	261,000
	———

Workings:

(W1) **Sales Return**

A sales return has not been accounted for. The correcting entry is:

Dr revenue	$500
Cr receivables	$500

(W2) **Cost of Sales**

	$
Opening inventory	24,000
Purchases	240,000
Depreciation	21,000
(($120,000 – $15,000) × 20%)	
Closing inventory	(30,000)
	———
	255,000
	———

(W3) **Administrative Expenses**

	$
Per trial balance	185,000
Irrecoverable debt	1,000
Provision	50,000
	———
	236,000
	———

(W4) **Receivables**

	$
Per trial balance	20,500
Allowance per trial balance	(2,000)
Irrecoverable debt	(1,000)
Sales return (W1)	(500)
	17,000

2   **WILLOW**

Statement of profit or loss and other comprehensive income for the year ended 30 June 20X1

	$000
Revenue	100,926
Cost of sales (W1)	(67,051)
Gross profit	33,875
Distribution costs (W2)	(7,826)
Administrative expenses (W3)	(11,761)
Profit from operations	14,288
Finance costs (W4)	(1,000)
Profit before taxation	13,288
Income tax expense	(2,700)
Profit for the year	10,588
Other comprehensive income for the year	
Gain on revaluation of the land (W5)	14,000
Total comprehensive income for the year	24,588

Statement of financial position as at 30 June 20X1

	$000
Non-current assets	
Property, plant and equipment (W6)	119,500
Current assets	
Inventories	9,420
Trade and other receivables (W7)	20,800
Cash and cash equivalents	2,213
Total assets	151,933

Equity

Share capital	50,000
Share premium	25,000
Retained earnings (W8)	20,508
Revaluation reserve ($10,000 + $14,000 (W5))	24,000

Non-current liabilities

5% bank loan	20,000

Current liabilities

Trade and other payables (W9)	9,725
Tax payable	2,700
	————
Equity and Liabilities	151,933
	————

Workings:

(W1) **Cost of sales**

	$000
Opening inventories	7,280
Purchases	67,231
Less closing inventories	(9,420)
Dep'n P&M ($2,800 (W4) × 70%)	1,960
	————
Total	67,051
	————

(W2) **Distribution costs**

	$000
Distribution costs	8,326
Dep'n P&M ($2,800 (W4) × 20%)	560
Advertising prepayment ($2,120 × 6/12)	(1,060)
	————
Total	7,826
	————

(W3) **Administrative expenses**

	$000
Administrative expenses	7,741
Depreciation Buildings (W4)	3,200
Dep'n P&M ($2,800 (W4) × 10%)	280
Irrecoverable debt	540
	————
Total	11,761
	————

(W4) **Finance costs**

	$000
Finance costs	0
Accrual for loan interest ($20,000 × 5%)	1,000
Total	1,000

(W5) **Revaluation**

	$000
Revalued amount	54,000
CV	40,000
Revaluation gain	14,000

(W6) **PPE**

	$000
Land and buildings cost	120,000
Revaluation	14,000
Accumulated depreciation	(22,500)
Depreciation charge (($120,000 − $40,000) × 4%)	(3,200)
Plant and equipment cost	32,000
Accumulated depreciation	(18,000)
Depreciation charge ($32,000 − $18,000) × 20%)	(2,800)
Total	119,500

(W7) **Trade and other receivables**

	$000
Trade and other receivables	20,280
Irrecoverable debt w/off	(540)
Advertising prepayment (W2)	1,060
Total	20,800

(W8) **Retained earnings**

	$000
Retained earnings	12,920
Profit per P/L	10,588
Dividends	(3,000)
Total	20,508

(W9) **Trade and other payables**

	$000
Trade and other payables	8,725
Accrual for loan interest (W4)	1,000
Total	9,725

3 CLERC

Statement of profit or loss and other comprehensive income for the year ended 31 December 20X9

	$
Revenue	178,833
Cost of sales (W1)	(146,920)
Gross profit	31,913
Distribution costs	(7,009)
Administrative expenses (W2)	(14,820)
Profit from operations	10,084
Investment income	100
Finance costs (W3)	(2,000)
Profit before taxation	8,184
Income tax expense	(7,162)
Profit for the year	1,022
Other comprehensive income for the year	
Gain on revaluation of the land (W4)	40,000
Total comprehensive income for the year	41,022

Statement of financial position as at 31 December 20X9

	$
Non-current assets	
Property, plant and equipment (W5)	267,592
Current assets	
Inventories (W1)	19,371
Trade and other receivables (W6)	7,032
Cash and cash equivalents	6,993
Total assets	300,988

EQUITY AND LIBILITIES	$
Equity	
Share capital	100,000
Share premium	20,000
Retained earnings (W7)	24,915
Revaluation reserve ($50,000 + $40,000 (W4))	90,000
Non-current liabilities	
Bank loans	40,000
Current liabilities	
Trade and other payables (W8)	18,911
Tax payable	7,162
Total equity and liabilities	300,988

Workings:

(W1) **Cost of sales**

	$
Opening inventories	17,331
Purchases	130,562
Less closing inventories	(19,371)
(19,871 – (4,000 – 3,500))	
Dep'n – building ($10,000 (W5) × 40%)	4,000
Dep'n – plant (W5)	14,398
Total	146,920

(W2) **Administrative expenses**

	$
Administrative expenses	7,100
Dep'n – building ($10,000 (W5) × 60%)	6,000
Irrecoverable debt w/off	1,720
Total	14,820

(W3) **Finance costs**

	$
Finance costs	0
Accrual for loan interest ($40,000 × 5%)	2,000
Total	2,000

(W4) **Revaluation of land**

	$
Revalued amount	150,000
CV	110,000
Revaluation gain	40,000

(W5) **PPE**

	$
Land and buildings cost	210,000
Revaluation	40,000
Accumulated depreciation	(30,000)
Dep'n charge (($210,000 – $110,000) × 10%)	(10,000)
Plant and machinery cost	88,000
Accumulated depreciation	(16,010)
Dep'n charge (($88,000 – $16,010) × 20%)	(14,398)
Total	267,592

(W6) **Trade and other receivables**

	$
Trade and other receivables	8,752
Irrecoverable debt w/off	(1,720)
Total	7,032

(W7) **Retained earnings**

	$
Retained earnings	23,893
Profit	1,022
Total	24,915

(W8) **Trade and other payables**

	$
Trade and other payables	13,882
Accruals ($3,029 + $2,000 (W3))	5,029
Total	18,911

4 CARBON

Statement of profit or loss for the year ended 31 December 20X5

	$
Revenue ($450,000 – $1,000 (W1))	449,000
Cost of sales (W2)	(210,000)
Gross profit	239,000
Administrative expenses (W3)	(162,500)
Distribution costs	(56,000)
Operating profit	20,500
Finance costs ($50,000 × 8% × 3/12)	(1,000)
Profit before tax	19,500
Income tax charge	(5,000)
Profit after taxation	14,500

Statement of financial position as at 31 December 20X5

	$
Non- current assets	
Property, plant and equipment	96,000
($150,000 – $30,000 – $24,000 (W2))	
Current assets	
Inventories	27,000
Receivables (W4)	30,000
Cash and cash equivalents	5,000
Total assets	158,000
Equity	
Ordinary share capital	10,000
Retained earnings ($25,500 + $14,500 (P/L)	40,000
Non-current liabilities	
8% Loan	50,000
Current liabilities	
Trade and other payables ($32,000 + $1,000 loan interest)	33,000
Tax payable	5,000
Provision	20,000
Total equity and liabilities	158,000

Workings:

(W1) **Sales Return**

A sales return has not been accounted for. The correcting entry is:

Dr revenue $1,000

Cr receivables $1,000 (W4)

(W2) **Cost of Sales**

	$
Opening inventory	33,000
Purchases	180,000
Depreciation	24,000
(($150,000 − $30,000) × 20%)	
Closing inventory	(27,000)
	210,000

(W3) **Administrative Expenses**

	$
Per trial balance	140,000
Irrecoverable debt (W4)	1,500
Increase in allowance for receivables (W4)	1,000
Provision – defective goods claim	20,000
	162,500

(W4) **Receivables**

	$
Per trial balance	36,000
Allowance per trial balance	(2,500)
Increase in allowance required (W3)	(1,000)
Irrecoverable debt (W3)	(1,500)
Sales return (W1)	(1,000)
	30,000

5   PATTY AND SELMA

(a) **Gross profit margin:**

Patty: (423/987) = 42.9%   Selma: (232/567) = 40.9%

Operating profit margin:

Patty: (200/987) = 20.3%   Selma: (110/567) = 19.4%

Interest cover:

Patty: (200/50) = 4.0   Selma: (110/30) = 3.7

(b) **Consolidated statement of profit or loss for year ended 31 December 20X1**

	$000
Revenue ($987 + $567 − $120)	1,434
Cost of sales ($564 + $335 −$120 + $5 (W1))	(784)
	———
Gross profit	650
Administrative expenses ($223 + $122)	(345)
	———
Operating profit	305
Finance costs ($50 + $30)	(80)
	———
Profit before taxation	225
Income tax expense ($40 + $25)	(65)
	———
Profit after tax	160
	———
Profit attributable to:	
Owners of Patty (bal fig)	145
Non-controlling interest (W2)	15
	———
	160
	———

Workings:

(W1) **PURP**

$120k/120 × 20 = $20k

The proportion of this profit remaining in inventory must be eliminated:

$20 × 25% = $5k

The double entry to adjust for this is:

Dr Cost of sales (P/L)	$5k
Cr Inventory (SFP)	$5k

(W2) **Non-controlling interest**

	$000	
NCI % of S's PAT (30% × $55k)		16.5
NCI % of PURP (30% × $5k (W1))	(1.5)	
	———	
	15	
	———	

6 CUBE AND PRISM

(a) **Quick ratio**

Cube: ($110 + $8)/$48 = 2.5   Prism: ($99 + $51)/$50 = 3.0

Gearing ratio

Cube: ($200/($100 + $435 + $200) = 27.2% Prism: ($70/($50 + $209 + $70) = 21.3%

(b) **Consolidated statement of financial position as at 31 December 20X1**

	$
Assets	
Non-current assets	
Property, plant and equipment ($270,000 + $179,000 + $70,000 FV uplift)	519,000
Goodwill (W3)	115,000
Current assets	
Inventories ($95,000 + $50,000 – $3,000 PURP (W6))	142,000
Trade and other receivables ($110,000 + $99,000)	209,000
Cash and cash equivalents ($8,000 + $51,000)	59,000
Total assets	1,044,000
Equity and liabilities	
Equity	
Share capital	100,000
Retained earnings (W5)	498,750
Non-controlling interest (W4)	77,250
Non-current liabilities	
Loans ($200,000 + $70,000)	270,000
Current liabilities	
Trade and other payables ($48,000 + $50,000)	98,000
Total equity and liabilities	1,044,000

Workings:

(W1) **Group structure**

Cube

75%

Prism

(W2) **Net assets of Prism**

	$ Reporting date	$ Acquisition	$ Post –acq
Share capital	50,000	50,000	
Retained earnings	209,000	120,000	
FV uplift ($170,000 – $100,000)	70,000	70,000	
	329,000	240,000	89,000

(W3) **Goodwill**

	$
Consideration	300,000
Less net assets at acquisition (W2)	(240,000)
Add NCI at acquisition	55,000
	115,000

(W4) **Non-controlling interest**

	$
NCI at acquisition	55,000
NCI % of Prism post-acquisition retained earnings (25% × $89,000 (W2))	22,250
	77,250

(W5) **Retained earnings**

	$
100% of Cube	435,000
PURP	(3,000)
75% of Prism post-acquisition retained earnings (75% × $89,000 (W2))	66,750
	498,750

(W6) **PURP**

Profit = $30,000 × 30% = $9,000

Profit remaining in group inventory = $9,000 × 1/3 = $3,000

The correcting entry is:

Dr Retained earnings (W5)	$3,000
Cr Inventories	$3,000

7   BRYSON AND STOPPARD

(a)   **Current ratio:**

Bryson: $5,760/$2,640 = 2.2

Stoppard: $5,010/$1,410 = 3.6

(b)   **Consolidated statement of financial position as at 31 March 20X1**

	$000
ASSETS	
Goodwill (W3)	4,450
Non-current assets ($11,280 + $3,670 + $1,000)	15,950
Current assets ($5,760 + $5,010 – $300 PURP (W6) – $480 intra-co)	9,990
Total assets	30,390
EQUITY AND LIABILITIES	
Equity	
Share capital	9,200
Retained earnings (W5)	12,645
Non-controlling interest (W4)	2,355
Non-current liabilities ($1,440 + $1,180)	2,620
Current liabilities ($2,640 + $1,410 – $480 intra-co)	3,570
Total equity and liabilities	30,390

(W1) **Group structure**

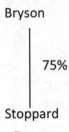

Bryson

75%

Stoppard

(W2)   **Net assets of Stoppard**

	$000 Reporting date	$000 Acquisition	$000 Post –acq
Share capital	4,800	4,800	
Retained earnings	1,290	670	
FV uplift	1,000	1,000	
	7,090	6,470	620

(W3) **Goodwill**

		$000
Consideration		8,720
FV of NCI at acquisition		2,200
Net assets at acquisition		(6,470)
Total		4,450

(W4) **Non-controlling interest**

	$000
NCI at acquisition	2,200
NCI % of Stoppard's post acquisition retained earnings ((25% × $620 (W2))	155
Total	2,355

(W5) **Retained earnings**

	$000
Bryson	12,480
PURP (W6)	(300)
Bryson's % of Stoppard's post acquisition retained earnings (75% × $ 620 (W2))	465
Total	12,645

(W6) **PURP**

Profit on intra-company sale = $400,000

Amount still in group inventory = $400,000 × ¾ = $300,000

The correcting entry is:

Dr Retained earnings (W5) $300,000

Cr Inventories $300,000

7   PEN AND STAPLE

(a)   **Gross profit margin:**

Pen: (725/1,500) = 48.3%   Staple: (330/700) = 47.1%

Operating profit margin:

Pen: (408/1,500) = 27.2%   Staple: (195/700) = 27.8%

Interest cover:

Pen: (408/60) = 6.8 times   Staple: (195/35) = 5.6 times

(b)   **Consolidated statement of profit or loss for year ended 31 December 20X4**

	$000
Revenue ($1,500 + $700 – $150 inter-co)	2,050
Cost of sales ($775 + $370 –$150 inter-co + $5 (W1))	(1,000)
Gross profit	1,050
Administrative expenses ($317 + $135)	(452)
Operating profit	598
Finance costs ($60 + $35)	(95)
Profit before taxation	503
Income tax expense ($96 + $45)	(141)
Profit after tax	362
Profit attributable to:	
Owners of Pen (bal fig)	329
Non-controlling interest (W2)	33
	362

(W1) **PURP**

$150,000 /120 × 20 = $25,000

The proportion of this profit remaining in inventory must be eliminated:

$25,000 × 1/5 = $5,000

The double entry to adjust for this is:

Dr Cost of sales (P/L) $5,000

Cr Inventory (SFP) $5,000

(W2) **Non-controlling interest**

	$000
NCI % of S's PAT (30% × $115,000)	34.5
NCI % of PURP (30% × $5,000 (W1))	(1.5)
	33

8   **PEBBLE AND STONE**

(a)   **Consolidated statement of financial position as at 31 December 20X6**

	$
Assets	
Non-current assets	
Property, plant & equip't ($300,000 + $225,000 + $30,000 FV adj)	555,000
Goodwill (W3)	230,000
Current assets	
Inventories ($80,000 + $75,000 – $5,000 PURP (W6))	150,000
Trade and other receivables ($60,000 + $140,000)	200,000
Cash and cash equivalents ($10,000 + $25,000)	35,000
	————
Total assets	1170,000
	————
Equity and liabilities	
Equity	
Share capital	80,000
Share premium	20,000
Retained earnings (W5)	370,000
Non-controlling interest (W4)	100,000
	————
Total equity of the group	570,000
Non-current liabilities	
Loans ($300,000 + $85,000)	385,000
Current liabilities	
Trade and other payables ($155,000 + $60,000)	215,000
	————
Total equity and liabilities	1,170,000
	————

(b)   Characteristics relevant to an investment in an associate are:

Significant influence over the activities of Archive

Ownership of between 20% and 50% of the ordinary shares of archive

Do not account for goodwill or recognise non-controlling interest as these are characteristics of accounting for a subsidiary where there is a relationship of control.

Workings:

(W1) **Group structure**

Pebble

80%

Stone

(W2) **Net assets of Stone**

	$ Reporting date	$ Acquisition	$ Post –acq
Share capital	60,000	60,000	
Share premium	10,000	10,000	
Retained earnings	250,000	150,000	
FV uplift ($180,000 – $150,000)	30,000	30,000	
	350,000	250,000	100,000

(W3) **Goodwill**

	$
Consideration	400,000
Add: NCI at acquisition	80,000
Less net assets at acquisition (W2)	(250,000)
	230,000

(W4) **Non-controlling interest**

	$
NCI at acquisition	80,000
NCI % of Stone post-acquisition retained earnings (20% × $100,000 (W2))	20,000
	100,000

(W5) **Retained earnings**

	$
100% of Pebble	295,000
PURP (W6)	(5000)
80% of Stone post-acquisition retained earnings (80% × $100,000 (W2))	80,000
	370,000

(W6) **PURP**

Profit = $50,000 × 25% = $12,500

Profit remaining in group inventory = $12,500 × 2/5 = $5,000

The correcting entry is:

Dr Retained earnings (W5)	$5,000
Cr Inventories (SOFP)	$5,000

Fundamentals Level – Knowledge Module

Financial Accounting

Specimen Exam applicable from June 2014

Time allowed: 2 hours

This paper is divided into two sections:

Section A – ALL 35 questions are compulsory and MUST
be attempted

Section B – BOTH questions are compulsory and MUST
be attempted

Do NOT open this paper until instructed by the supervisor.

This question paper must not be removed from the examination hall.

The Association of Chartered Certified Accountants

Section A – ALL 35 questions are compulsory and MUST be attempted

Please use the space provided on the inside cover of the Candidate Answer Booklet to indicate your chosen answer to each multiple choice question.
Each question is worth 2 marks.

1 **Which of the following calculates a sole trader's net profit for a period?**

   A Closing net assets + drawings – capital introduced – opening net assets
   B Closing net assets – drawings + capital introduced – opening net assets
   C Closing net assets – drawings – capital introduced – opening net assets
   D Closing net assets + drawings + capital introduced – opening net assets

2 **Which of the following explains the imprest system of operating petty cash?**

   A Weekly expenditure cannot exceed a set amount
   B The exact amount of expenditure is reimbursed at intervals to maintain a fixed float
   C All expenditure out of the petty cash must be properly authorised
   D Regular equal amounts of cash are transferred into petty cash at intervals

3 **Which of the following statements are TRUE of limited liability companies?**

   (1) The company's exposure to debts and liability is limited
   (2) Financial statements must be produced
   (3) A company continues to exist regardless of the identity of its owners

   A 1 and 2 only
   B 1 and 3 only
   C 2 and 3 only
   D 1, 2 and 3

4 Annie is a sole trader who does not keep full accounting records. The following details relate to her transactions with credit customers and suppliers for the year ended 30 June 20X6:

	$
Trade receivables, 1 July 20X5	130,000
Trade payables, 1 July 20X5	60,000
Cash received from customers	686,400
Cash paid to suppliers	(302,800)
Discounts allowed	1,400
Discounts received	(2,960)
Contra between payables and receivables ledgers	(2,000)
Trade receivables, 30 June 20X6	181,000
Trade payables, 30 June 20X6	(84,000)

What figure should appear for purchases in Annie's statement of profit or loss for the year ended 30 June 20X6?

   A $325,840
   B $330,200
   C $331,760
   D $327,760

5 Which TWO of the following errors would cause the total of the debit column and the total of the credit column of a trial balance not to agree?

   (1) A transposition error was made when entering a sales invoice into the sales day book
   (2) A cheque received from a customer was credited to cash and correctly recognised in receivables
   (3) A purchase of non-current assets was omitted from the accounting records
   (4) Rent received was included in the trial balance as a debit balance

   A   1 and 2
   B   1 and 3
   C   2 and 3
   D   2 and 4

6 At 31 December 20X5 the following require inclusion in a company's financial statements:

   (1) On 1 January 20X5 the company made a loan of $12,000 to an employee, repayable on 1 January 20X6, charging interest at 2% per year. On the due date she repaid the loan and paid the whole of the interest due on the loan to that date.
   (2) The company paid an annual insurance premium of $9,000 in 20X5, covering the year ending 31 August 20X6.
   (3) In January 20X6 the company received rent from a tenant of $4,000 covering the six months to 31 December 20X5.

   For these items, what total figures should be included in the company's statement of financial position as at 31 December 20X5?

   A   Current assets $10,000   Current liabilities $12,240
   B   Current assets $22,240   Current liabilities $nil
   C   Current assets $10,240   Current liabilities $nil
   D   Current assets $16,240   Current liabilities $6,000

7 A company's statement of profit or loss for the year ended 31 December 20X5 showed a net profit of $83,600. It was later found that $18,000 paid for the purchase of a motor van had been debited to the motor expenses account. It is the company's policy to depreciate motor vans at 25% per year on the straight line basis, with a full year's charge in the year of acquisition.

   What would the net profit be after adjusting for this error?

   A $106,100
   B $70,100
   C $97,100
   D $101,600

8 Xena has the following working capital ratios:

	20X9	20X8
Current ratio	1·2:1	1·5:1
Receivables days	75 days	50 days
Payables days	30 days	45 days
Inventory turnover	42 days	35 days

   Which of the following statements is correct?

   A   Xena's liquidity and working capital has improved in 20X9
   B   Xena is receiving cash from customers more quickly in 20X9 than in 20X8
   C   Xena is suffering from a worsening liquidity position in 20X9
   D   Xena is taking longer to pay suppliers in 20X9 than in 20X8

9 Which of the following statements is/are correct?

(1) A statement of cash flows prepared using the direct method produces a different figure to net cash from operating activities from that produced if the indirect method is used
(2) Rights issues of shares do not feature in a statement of cash flows
(3) A surplus on revaluation of a non-current asset will not appear as an item in a statement of cash flows
(4) A profit on the sale of a non-current asset will appear as an item under cash flows from investing activities in the statement of cash flows

A 1 and 3 only
B 3 and 4 only
C 2 and 4 only
D 3 only

10 A company receives rent from a large number of properties. The total received in the year ended 30 April 20X6 was $481,200.

The following were the amounts of rent in advance and in arrears at 30 April 20X5 and 20X6:

	30 April 20X5	30 April 20X6
	$	$
Rent received in advance	28,700	31,200
Rent in arrears (all subsequently received)	21,200	18,400

What amount of rental income should appear in the company's statement of profit or loss for the year ended 30 April 20X6?

A $486,500
B $460,900
C $501,500
D $475,900

11 Which of the following are differences between sole traders and limited liability companies?

(1) A sole trader's financial statements are private and never made available to third parties; a company's financial statements are sent to shareholders and may be publicly filed
(2) Only companies have share capital
(3) A sole trader is fully and personally liable for any losses that the business might make
(4) Drawings would only appear in the financial statements of a sole trader

A 1 and 4 only
B 2, 3 and 4
C 2 and 3 only
D 1, 3 and 4

12 Which of the following statements is true?

A The interpretation of an entity's financial statements using ratios is only useful for potential investors
B Ratios based on historical data can predict the future performance of an entity
C The analysis of financial statements using ratios provides useful information when compared with previous performance or industry averages
D An entity's management will not assess an entity's performance using financial ratios

13 A company's motor vehicles cost account at 30 June 20X6 is as follows:

Motor vehicles – cost

	$		$
Balance b/f	35,800	Disposal	12,000
Additions	12,950	Balance c/f	36,750
	48,750		48,750

What opening balance should be included in the following period's trial balance for Motor vehicles – cost at 1 July 20X6?

A $36,750 Dr
B $48,750 Dr
C $36,750 Cr
D $48,750 Cr

14 Which TWO of the following items must be disclosed in the note to the financial statements for intangible assets?

(1) The useful lives of intangible assets capitalised in the financial statements
(2) A description of the development projects that have been undertaken during the period
(3) A list of all intangible assets purchased or developed in the period
(4) Impairment losses written off intangible assets during the period

A   1 and 4
B   2 and 3
C   3 and 4
D   1 and 2

15 Which of the following statements are correct?

(1) Capitalised development expenditure must be amortised over a period not exceeding five years.
(2) Capitalised development costs are shown in the statement of financial position under the heading of non-current assets
(3) If certain criteria are met, research expenditure must be recognised as an intangible asset.

A   2 only
B   2 and 3
C   1 only
D   1 and 3

16 The following transactions relate to Rashid's electricity expense ledger account for the year ended 30 June 20X9:

	$
Prepayment brought forward	550
Cash paid	5,400
Accrual carried forward	650

What amount should be charged to the statement of profit or loss in the year ended 30 June 20X9 for electricity?

A $6,600
B $5,400
C $5,500
D $5,300

17 At 30 June 20X5 a company's allowance for receivables was $39,000. At 30 June 20X6 trade receivables totalled $517,000. It was decided to write off debts totalling $37,000 and to adjust the allowance for receivables to the equivalent of 5% of the trade receivables based on past events.

What figure should appear in the statement of profit or loss for the year ended 30 June 20X6 for receivables expense?

- **A** $61,000
- **B** $52,000
- **C** $22,000
- **D** $37,000

18 The total of the list of balances in Valley's payables ledger was $438,900 at 30 June 20X6. This balance did not agree with Valley's payables ledger control account balance. The following errors were discovered:

(1) A contra entry of $980 was recorded in the payables ledger control account, but not in the payables ledger.
(2) The total of the purchase returns daybook was undercast by $1,000.
(3) An invoice for $4,344 was posted to the supplier's account as $4,434.

What amount should Valley report in its statement of financial position for accounts payable at 30 June 20X6?

- **A** $436,830
- **B** $438,010
- **C** $439,790
- **D** $437,830

19 **According to IAS 2 *Inventories*, which TWO of the following costs should be included in valuing the inventories of a manufacturing company?**

(1) Carriage inwards
(2) Carriage outwards
(3) Depreciation of factory plant
(4) General administrative overheads

- **A** 1 and 4
- **B** 1 and 3
- **C** 3 and 4
- **D** 2 and 3

20 Prisha has not kept accurate accounting records during the financial year. She had opening inventory of $6,700 and purchased goods costing $84,000 during the year. At the year end she had $5,400 left in inventory. All sales are made at a mark up on cost of 20%.

What is Prisha's gross profit for the year?

- **A** $13,750
- **B** $17,060
- **C** $16,540
- **D** $20,675

21 At 31 December 20X4 a company's capital structure was as follows:

$

Ordinary share capital   125,000
(500,000 shares of 25c each)
Share premium account   100,000

In the year ended 31 December 20X5 the company made a rights issue of 1 share for every 2 held at $1 per share and this was taken up in full. Later in the year the company made a bonus issue of 1 share for every 5 held, using the share premium account for the purpose.

What was the company's capital structure at 31 December 20X5?

	Ordinary share capital	Share premium account
A	$450,000	$25,000
B	$225,000	$250,000
C	$225,000	$325,000
D	$212,500	$262,500

22 Which of the following should appear in a company's statement of changes in equity?

(1) Total comprehensive income for the year
(2) Amortisation of capitalised development costs
(3) Surplus on revaluation of non-current assets

A   1, 2 and 3
B   2 and 3 only
C   1 and 3 only
D   1 and 2 only

23 The plant and machinery account (at cost) of a business for the year ended 31 December 20X5 was as follows:

Plant and machinery – cost

20X5		$	20X5		$
1 Jan	Balance b/f	240,000	31 Mar	Transfer to disposal account	60,000
30 Jun	Cash purchase of plant	160,000	31 Dec	Balance c/f	340,000
		400,000			400,000

The company's policy is to charge depreciation at 20% per year on the straight line basis, with proportionate depreciation in the years of purchase and disposal.

What should be the depreciation charge for the year ended 31 December 20X5?

A $68,000
B $64,000
C $61,000
D $55,000

7

[P.T.O.

24 The following extracts are from Hassan's financial statements:

	$
Profit before interest and tax	10,200
Interest	(1,600)
Tax	(3,300)
Profit after tax	5,300
Share capital	20,000
Reserves	15,600
	35,600
Loan liability	6,900
	42,500

What is Hassan's return on capital employed?

A 15%
B 29%
C 24%
D 12%

25 Which of the following statements about sales tax is/are true?

(1) Sales tax is an expense to the ultimate consumer of the goods purchased
(2) Sales tax is recorded as income in the accounts of the entity selling the goods

A 1 only
B 2 only
C Both 1 and 2
D Neither 1 nor 2

26 Q's trial balance failed to agree and a suspense account was opened for the difference. Q does not keep receivables and payables control accounts. The following errors were found in Q's accounting records:

(1) In recording an issue of shares at par, cash received of $333,000 was credited to the ordinary share capital account as $330,000
(2) Cash of $2,800 paid for plant repairs was correctly accounted for in the cash book but was credited to the plant asset account
(3) The petty cash book balance of $500 had been omitted from the trial balance
(4) A cheque for $78,400 paid for the purchase of a motor car was debited to the motor vehicles account as $87,400.

Which of the errors will require an entry to the suspense account to correct them?

A 1, 2 and 4 only
B 1, 2, 3 and 4
C 1 and 4 only
D 2 and 3 only

27 Prior to the financial year end of 31 July 20X9, Cannon Co has received a claim of $100,000 from a supplier for providing poor quality goods which have damaged the supplier's plant and equipment. Cannon Co's lawyers have stated that there is a 20% chance that Cannon will successfully defend the claim.

Which of the following is the correct accounting treatment for the claim in the financial statements for the year ended 31 July 20X9?

A   Cannon should neither provide for nor disclose the claim
B   Cannon should disclose a contingent liability of $100,000
C   Cannon should provide for the expected cost of the claim of $100,000
D   Cannon should provide for an expected cost of $20,000

28 Gareth, a sales tax registered trader purchased a computer for use in his business. The invoice for the computer showed the following costs related to the purchase:

	$
Computer	890
Additional memory	95
Delivery	10
Installation	20
Maintenance (1 year)	25
	1,040
Sales tax (17·5%)	182
Total	1,222

How much should Gareth capitalise as a non-current asset in relation to the purchase?

A $1,193
B $1,040
C $1,222
D $1,015

29 The following bank reconciliation statement has been prepared by a trainee accountant:

	$
Overdraft per bank statement	(3,860)
Less: Unpresented cheques	(9,160)
	5,300
Add: Outstanding lodgements	16,690
Cash at bank	21,990

What should be the correct balance per the cash book?

A $21,990 balance at bank as stated
B $3,670 balance at bank
C $11,390 balance at bank
D $3,670 overdrawn

[P.T.O.

30 The IASB's *Conceptual Framework for Financial Reporting* identifies characteristics which make financial information faithfully represent what it purports to represent.

Which of the following are examples of those characteristics?

(1) Accruals
(2) Completeness
(3) Going concern
(4) Neutrality

A   1 and 2
B   2 and 4
C   2 and 3
D   1 and 4

31 The following control account has been prepared by a trainee accountant:

Receivables ledger control account

	$		$
Opening balance	308,600	Cash	147,200
Credit sales	154,200	Discounts allowed	1,400
Cash sales	88,100	Interest charged on overdue accounts	2,400
Contras	4,600	Irrecoverable debts	4,900
		Allowance for receivables	2,800
		Closing balance	396,800
	555,500		555,500

What should the closing balance be when all the errors made in preparing the receivables ledger control account have been corrected?

A $395,200
B $304,300
C $309,500
D $307,100

32 **Which of the following material events after the reporting date and before the financial statements are approved are adjusting events?**

(1) A valuation of property providing evidence of impairment in value at the reporting date.
(2) Sale of inventory held at the reporting date for less than cost.
(3) Discovery of fraud or error affecting the financial statements.
(4) The insolvency of a customer with a debt owing at the reporting date which is still outstanding.

A   1, 2 and 4 only
B   1, 2, 3 and 4
C   1 and 4 only
D   2 and 3 only

33 A company values its inventory using the FIFO method. At 1 May 20X5 the company had 700 engines in inventory, valued at $190 each. During the year ended 30 April 20X6 the following transactions took place:

20X5
1 July	Purchased 500 engines at $220 each
1 November	Sold 400 engines for $160,000

20X6
1 February	Purchased 300 engines at $230 each
15 April	Sold 250 engines for $125,000

What is the value of the company's closing inventory of engines at 30 April 20X6?

A $188,500
B $195,500
C $166,000
D $106,000

34 Amy is a sole trader and had assets of $569,400 and liabilities of $412,840 on 1 January 20X8. During the year ended 31 December 20X8 she paid $65,000 capital into the business and she paid herself wages of $800 per month.

At 31 December 20X8, Amy had assets of $614,130 and liabilities of $369,770.

What is Amy's profit for the year ended 31 December 20X8?

A $32,400
B $23,600
C $22,800
D $87,800

35 Bumbly Co extracted the trial balance for the year ended 31 December 20X7. The total of the debits exceeded the credits by $300.

Which of the following could explain the imbalance?

A   Sales of $300 were omitted from the sales day book
B   Returns inward of $150 were extracted to the debit column of the trial balance
C   Discounts received of $150 were extracted to the debit column of the trial balance
D   The bank ledger account did not agree with the bank statement by a debit of $300

(70 marks)

[P.T.O.

Section B – BOTH questions are compulsory and MUST be attempted

Please write your answer within the answer booklet in accordance with the detailed instructions provided within each of the questions in this section of the exam paper.

1 Keswick Co acquired 80% of the share capital of Derwent Co on 1 June 20X5. The summarised draft statements of profit or loss for Keswick Co and Derwent Co for the year ended 31 May 20X6 are shown below:

	Keswick Co $000	Derwent Co $000
Revenue	8,400	3,200
Cost of sales	(4,600)	(1,700)
Gross profit	3,800	1,500
Operating expenses	(2,200)	(960)
Profit before tax	1,600	540
Tax	(600)	(140)
Profit for the year	1,000	400

[handwritten annotations: 1500; −1500 + 150; 10,400; 4,950; 5,150]

During the year Keswick Co sold goods costing $1,000,000 to Derwent Co for $1,500,000. At 31 May 20X6, 30% of these goods remained in Derwent Co's inventory.

Required:

(a) **Prepare the Keswick group consolidated statement of profit or loss for the year ended 31 May 20X6.**

Note: The statement should stop once the consolidated profit for the year has been determined. The amounts attributable to the non-controlling interest and equity owners of Keswick are not required. Show all workings as credit will be awarded to these as appropriate. (7 marks)

(b) **Which of the following formulas describes the amount to be entered in the consolidated statement of profit or loss as 'Profit attributable to: Equity owners of Keswick Co'?**

A   Group profit after tax – non-controlling interest
B   Group profit after tax + non-controlling interest
C   Keswick Co's profit after tax
D   Group profit after tax

(2 marks)

(c) **What amount should be shown in the consolidated statement of profit or loss for the non-controlling interest?**

(2 marks)

[handwritten: 400 × 20% = 80]

(d) The following table shows factors to be considered when determining whether a parent–subsidiary relationship exists.

Factor	Description
A	Significant influence
B	Control
C	Non-controlling interest
D	Greater than 50% of the equity shares being held by an investor
E	100% of the equity shares being held by an investor
F	Greater than 50% of the preference shares being held by an investor
G	50% of all shares and all debt being held by an investor
H	Greater than 50% of preference shares and debt being held by an investor

Required:

Which of the above factors A to H illustrate the existence of a parent–subsidiary relationship? (4 marks)

(15 marks)

2 Malright, a limited liability company, has an accounting year end of 31 October. The accountant is preparing the financial statements as at 31 October 20X7 and requires your assistance. The following trial balance has been extracted from the general ledger

Account	Dr $000	Cr $000
Buildings at cost	740	
Buildings accumulated depreciation, 1 November 20X6		60
Plant at cost	220	
Plant accumulated depreciation, 1 November 20X6		110
Bank balance		70
Revenue		1,800
Net purchases	1,140	
Inventory at 1 November 20X6	160	
Cash	20	
Trade payables		250
Trade receivables	320	
Administrative expenses	325	
Allowance for receivables at 1 November 20X6		10
Retained earnings at 1 November 20X6		130
Equity shares, $1		415
Share premium account		80
	2,925	2,925

The following additional information is also available:

– The allowance for receivables is to be increased to 5% of trade receivables. The allowance for receivables is treated as an administrative expense.

– Plant is depreciated at 20% per annum using the reducing balance method and buildings are depreciated at 5% per annum on their original cost. Depreciation is treated as a cost of sales expense.

– Closing inventory has been counted and is valued at $75,000.

– An invoice of $15,000 for energy costs relating to the quarter ended 30 November 20X7 was received on 2 December 20X7. Energy costs are included in administrative expenses.

Required:

Prepare the statement of profit or loss and the statement of financial position of Malright Co as at 31 October 20X7.

(15 marks)

End of Question Paper

Answers

Section A

1   A

2   B

3   C

4   C

Payables:	$
Balance b/f	60,000
Cash paid to suppliers	(302,800)
Discounts received	(2,960)
Contra	(2,000)
Balance c/f	(84,000)
Purchases	331,760

5   D

6   B

Current assets	$
Loan asset	12,000
Interest (12,000 x 12%)	240
Prepayment (8/12 x 9,000)	6,000
Accrued rent	4,000
	22,240

7   C

	$
Profit	83,600
Purchase of van	18,000
Depreciation 18,000 x 25%	(4,500)
	97,100

8   C

9   D

10 D

	$
Balance b/f (advance)	28,700
Balance b/f (arrears)	(21,200)
Cash received	481,200
Balance c/f (advance)	(31,200)
Balance c/f (arrears)	18,400
	475,900

11 B

12 C

13 A

14 A

15 A

16 A

	$
Balance b/f	550
Expense incurred (cash)	5,400
Accrual c/f	650
	6,600

17 C

	$	$
Debts written off		37,000
Movement in allowance:		
(517 – 37) x 5%	24,000	
Less opening allowance	39,000	
		(15,000)
Receivables expense		22,000

18 D

	$
Balance per ledger	438,900
Less contra	(980)
Posting error	(90)
Corrected balance	437,830

19 B

20 B

(6,700 + 84,000 – 5,400) x 20% = $17,060

21 B

	Share capital	Share premium
	$	$
Balance b/f	125,000	100,000
Rights issue	62,500	187,500
Bonus issue	37,500	(37,500)
Balance c/f	225,000	250,000

22 C

23 D

Depreciation:

		$
Jan–Mar	240,000 x 20% x 3/12	12,000
Apr–Jun	(240,000 – 60,000) x 20% x 3/12	9,000
Jul–Dec	(180,000 + 160,000) x 20% x 6/12	34,000
		55,000

24 C

10,200/42,500

25 A

26 B

27 C

28 D

1,040 – 25 = $1,015

29 B

	$
Overdraft per bank statement	(3,860)
Less: Unpresented cheques	(9,160)
Add: Outstanding lodgements	16,690
Cash at bank	3,670

30 B

31 D

Receivables ledger control account

	$		$
Opening balance	308,600	Cash	147,200
Credit sales	154,200	Discounts allowed	1,400
Interest charged on overdue accounts	2,400	Contras	4,600
		Irrecoverable debts	4,900
		Closing balance	307,100
	465,200		465,200

32 B

33 A

Closing inventory:

	$
50 x $190	9,500
500 x $220	110,000
300 x $230	69,000
	188,500

34 A

	$
Opening assets	569,400
Opening liabilities	(412,840)
Capital introduced	65,000
Drawings (800 x 12)	(9,600)
	211,960
Profit (bal fig)	32,400
Closing net assets (614,130 – 369,770)	244,360

35 C

Section B

1 (a) Consolidated statement of profit or loss for the year ended 31 May 20X6

	$000
Revenue (W1)	10,100
Cost of sales (W1)	(4,950)
Gross profit	5,150
Operating expenses (W1)	(3,160)
Profit before tax	1,990
Tax (W1)	(740)
Profit for the year	1,250

(b) A

(c) Non-controlling interest = $80,000 ($400,000 (W1) x 20%)

(d) The following factors illustrate the existence of a parent–subsidiary relationship: B, C, D, E.

Workings

Working 1

	Keswick Co $000	Derwent Co $000	Adjustments $000	Consolidated $000
Revenue	8,400	3,200	(1,500)	10,100
Cost of sales	(4,600)	(1,700)	1,500	(4,950)
Unrealised profit	(150)			
Operating expenses	(2,200)	(960)		(3,160)
Tax	(600)	(140)		(740)
	850	400		

2 Statement of profit or loss for the year ended 31 October 20X7

	$000
Revenue	1,800
Cost of sales (W1)	(1,284)
Gross profit	516
Administrative expenses (325 + 10 (W4) + (16 (W3) – 10))	(341)
Profit for the year	175

Statement of financial position as at 31 October 20X7

	$000	$000
Assets		
Non-current assets (W2)		731
Current assets		
Inventories	75	
Trade receivables (W3)	304	
Cash	20	
		399
Total assets		1,130
Equity and liabilities		
Equity		
Share capital	415	
Retained earnings (130 + 175)	305	
Share premium	80	
		800
Current liabilities		
Trade and other payables (250 + 10 (W4))	260	
Bank overdraft	70	
		330
Total equity and liabilities		1,130

Workings

Working 1

	$000
Cost of sales	
Opening inventory	160
Purchases	1,140
Closing inventory	(75)
	1,225
Depreciation (W2)	59
	1,284

Working 2

	Property $000	Plant $000	Total $000
Cost	740	220	960
Depreciation b/f	(60)	(110)	(170)
Depreciation for year			
740 x 5%	(37)		
(220 − 110) x 20%		(22)	(59)
Net book value 31 October 20X7	643	88	731

Working 3

Trade receivables
Allowance = 320,000 x 5% = $16,000
320,000 − 16,000 = $304,000

Working 4

Energy cost accrual
15,000 x 2/3 = $10,000

Fundamentals Level – Knowledge Module, Paper F3
Financial Accounting

Specimen Exam Marking Scheme

Marks

1 **(a)** Format of consolidated statement of profit or loss — 1
Revenue — 2
Cost of sales — 2
Operating expenses — 1
Tax expense — 1
___
7

(b) — 2

(c) — 2

(d) — 4
___
15
___

2 Formats — 1

Statement of profit or loss
Revenue — 0·5
Cost of sales — 3·5
Administrative expenses — 2·5

Statement of financial position
Non-current assets — 1
Inventory — 0·5
Receivables — 1·5
Cash — 0·5
Share capital — 0·5
Retained earnings — 1·5
Share premium — 0·5
Payables — 1
Overdraft — 0·5
___
15
___